Revised and Updated

Lyssa Royal ✦ Keith Priest

the PRISM of LYRA

An
Exploration
of Human
Galactic Heritage

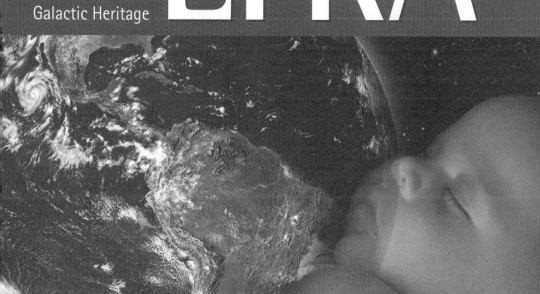

Other Publications by
Lyssa Royal

Preparing for Contact
Galactic Roots Cards

the PRISM of LYRA

An Exploration of Human Galactic Heritage

Lyssa Royal ✦ Keith Priest

3 LIGHT Technology
PUBLISHING

© 2011 by Royal Priest Research
All rights reserved.

No part of this book may be used or reproduced in any manner without prior
written permission from the publisher, except in the case of brief
quotations embodied in critical reviews and articles.

The scanning, uploading, and distribution of this text via the Internet or
via any other means without the permission of the publisher is illegal and pun-
ishable by law.   Please purchase only authorized electronic editions,
and do not participate in or encourage electronic piracy of copyrighted
materials. Your support of the author's rights is appreciated.

*   *   *

ISBN-13: 978-1-891824-87-6

Chapter illustrations:
Michael Z. Tyree

Light Technology Publishing, LLC
Phone: 800-450-0985
Fax: 928-714-1132
PO Box 3540
Flagstaff, AZ 86003
www.lighttechnology.com

Table of Contents

To the children of Lyra scattered throughout the galxy near and far . . . may you remember your heritage.

Preface

This book was first published in 1989 by Light Technology Publishing. At the time, it was one of the first of its kind that explored Earth's connection with the stars in a profound and meaningful way. Since then, it was republished by Royal Priest Research Press and translated into many languages worldwide. Now we have come full circle with this release of Volume 2 of *The Prism of Lyra*, once again published by Light Technology. This classic book has been the foundation of our work since the late 1980s and for many years we have wished to release a revised edition with added information. Finally, that day is here.

Part I of this book contains the original material from *The Prism of Lyra* without any changes except slight editorial ones. Since the material was dictated from the multidimensional consciousness Germane, channeled in 1989 through Lyssa Royal Holt, we did not wish to change anything.

Part II of this book is a transcript, edited for clarity, from a workshop given by Lyssa channeling Germane, in Grass Valley, CA in 1999. Considering the many hours of channeled material Lyssa has channeled on this subject from the 1980s to present day (and listening to feedback from devoted students), we felt this was the most comprehensive session that would be a perfect choice for the revised edition.

Recognizing our connection to the stars is more important now than ever before. It is one of the biggest shifts in consciousness our planet can undergo that will propel us toward creating a planetary community—

something we desperately need in this time of chaos. It is our hope that this book can assist that process, if even in a small way. Thank you for your heartfelt interest. To the children of Lyra scattered throughout the galaxy . . . may you remember your heritage!

Acknowledgments

Part I

This manuscript came about mostly because it was the kind of book we were searching for during the 1980s. Since it wasn't available, we wrote it! We thank all those who also searched and then lovingly inspired us to create it.

We thank channel and friend Darryl Anka (and Bashar) for providing the initial inspiration in 1985 to begin the search for this complex yet intriguing information. The integrity he possesses and the quality of his channeling inspired our confidence that we could reliably obtain this information.

We thank channel Robert Shapiro for providing some unique and elusive information regarding the Zeta Reticuli and the negative Sirians. Robert has the courage to tackle areas as a channel that many individuals are not willing to approach.

We thank author Barbara Hand Clow for offering valuable feedback and encouragement during revisions of the manuscript. Her enthusiastic responses to our work helped perpetuate our momentum and focus us at the moments we valued it most.

We thank Michael Z. Tyree for his sharp intuitive sense in creating the chapter artwork that expresses the deep symbolism of this information.

We send love and thanks to the Thursday evening group for sitting through eight weeks of Sedona's record-breaking heat in the summer of 1989 in order to delve more deeply into the extraterrestrial issue by utilizing the channeling process of Lyssa Royal.

We thank friend Jeannine Calaba for her detailed and insightful critique of the first draft. Her love, friendship, and support have been invaluable to the project.

We thank the late Margaret Pinyon for her highly professional editing and proofreading. She has taught us more about writing and sentence structure than anyone on Earth!

We thank Stacey Vornbrock for pointing out awkwardness and offering suggestions on a most difficult section of the book . . . and for the coconut cake!

Part II

Our thanks go to many people who, over the years, have encouraged this work and asked for more. Special thanks go to Bill Getman, who suggested the material to be used for Part II when we found it hard to choose from hundreds of hours of material. His wisdom and guidance are most cherished and appreciated.

We cannot forget the multidimensional consciousness Germane, who provided most of the information in this book and subsequent workshops, books, and channeled material for more than twenty years. In 2010 he pushed us to create the *Galactic Heritage Cards*, a 108-card divination system that assists seekers in processing this deep information and applying it in their own lives. He continually amazes us with his profound insights and depth of understanding about our universe.

Finally, we thank all of our readers and students around the world in many countries who have kept interest in this classic book alive. Without you, this revised edition would never have been born. Thank you for your encouragement, your letters, and your passion regarding this subject matter. This book is for you!

Download mp3 channeled sessions
Read free transcripts
Join our mailing list at:
www.lyssaroyal.com

Introduction

*It was not the mixture, O men, of blood and breath
that made the beginning and
substance of your souls, though your earthborn
and mortal body is framed of those things.
But your soul has come hither from another place.*

—Empedocles

From the earliest days in Earth's recorded history, there has been a bittersweet emotion that wells up within us as we gaze into the expanse of the night sky. Some of us long for the day when the human race can travel beyond the stars. Is it really just a hope for the future rather than a remembrance of our past?

The human consciousness has intricacies that still remain unexplored. What stirs us to push evolution to its limits? What drives us to create dissension between the races on our planet? Perhaps it is possible that we are playing out a cosmic drama and have only temporarily forgotten the script. We know that what one country or race does upon the Earth affects another. This idea may also spread outward into the universe. Perhaps what we do here affects countless other civilizations on other planets. Could we really be that linked together?

The information presented in this book is a compilation of years of insights, deductive reasoning, and channeling. Meticulous cross referencing of various channels has been conducted (primarily using the work of co-author Lyssa Royal), as well as research into a number of respected anthropological and metaphysical works. The reader may consider these ideas to be literal or symbolic, for the story is the same. There is no claim that this is the ultimate truth of our galactic family's emergence into this reality. If it works for you, use the insights given here as a catalyst for your own growth. If not, perhaps it can lead you one step closer to your own personal truth.

One of the most important ideas to accelerate the human potential is the allowance of all truths to be a manifestation of the One Truth, whatever it may be. Through this allowance emerges unification. If nothing else, let this book be fun to read, interesting, and stimulating to your imagination. Your belief is certainly not required—but your willingness to be an explorer is!

This is an introductory book. An extensive glossary has been created at the end of the material for any unfamiliar terms that may have been used. Each chapter represents a different facet of an intricate tapestry and how the tapestry affects Earth. Through many discussions, the information has been honed down into a framework that will introduce the reader to a cast of characters. The cast is not complete. There are countless other members and dramas being played out throughout our universe. These characters have emerged as the ones who seem to matter most to the human drama here on Earth.

There are certain assumptions carried throughout the material that are a foundation for the rest of the information. One of these is the idea of reincarnation and the infinite nature of consciousness. It is not necessary to embrace this concept in order to grasp the material, but it will allow the reader a more expanded view of the bigger picture.

Another assumption presented is the idea that each being possesses a higher awareness. It is purported that regardless of the level of existence a being has chosen for a given lifetime, it retains an awareness (conscious or subconscious) of its connection to the Whole and its divine identity. This concept connects us with the idea that it is *we and we alone* who control our destinies. Therefore, evolution is in our own hands.

Throughout the entire book the assumption will also be carried that the "Whole," or the integrated mass consciousness of our galactic family, has always existed. For the purposes of the information presented, there will need to be some set parameters. These parameters will allegorically refer to the "beginning" of the story as being the *Dimensional Infusion* and the "end" as the *Integration*.

In many cases labels have been used to denote places or people (such as Sirius, or Sirians). In general, these labels are fluid, more denoting a *realm* or *vibrational awareness* than a fixed idea. In a case such as Lyra, for example, the possibility is respected that the very stars spoken of have become black holes and white holes many times over. Therefore, these can be spoken of as *ideas* rather than concrete points in time and space. These ideas carry weight; this is quite apparent in our legends that give importance to other star systems. The Dogon tribe legends, the Sumerian Texts, and the ancient Egyptian writings all claim contact with beings from other star systems. These legends must come from *somewhere*. Though their language and contemporary style of expression differ slightly, the consistency of their content is beyond argument.

Information about the past of the human race can enrich our lives *here* on Earth. If we are to truly transform, it will be through the infusing of awareness onto our world, *not* using the awareness to escape from our responsibilities as citizens of Earth and the Galactic Family.

Note: Please read the footnotes *and* the glossary! ☺

"I am a child of Earth and starry Heaven;
But my race is of Heaven alone.
This ye know yourselves. . . "

—Translated from the Petelia Plate
Orphic Initiates, 200–400 b.c.

Part 1

1

Dimensional Infusion

With its celestial keys,
Its chords of air, its frets of fire,
The Samian's great Aeolian Lyre,
Rising through all its sevenfold bars,
From Earth unto the fixed stars.

—Longfellow on Lyra from *Occultation of Orion*

All consciousness and energy was once fused into an integrated whole. This Whole was aware of aspects of itself, but in a different way from individualized consciousness. In Earth's present development the self is recognized first, then society, and finally the Whole, All That Is, or God. Separation is still created. This separation from the Source is an illusion. This illusion is a tool that provides the Whole with all the necessary lessons and challenges it needs to experience in order to reintegrate back into the Source.

Before this fragmentation from the Source, the Whole existed in another octave of dimensional reality. From this realm of unification, portions of All That Is wondered what it would be like to fragment and temporarily forget integrated existence. The force of this thought on such a mass level began to create a fragmentation. The illusion created from this fragmentation would be a challenging forgetfulness in which consciousness would need to create (from its own divine nature) the remembrance to once again unite.

What has been termed *"creation"* is indeed this fragmentation, or, more descriptively, the *Dimensional Infusion*. The Whole's initial curiosity about a fragmented existence actually *created* the reality itself. It required a shift in perspective, focus, or frequency. As part of the Whole, aspects of the Galactic Family were partially responsible for laying out the blueprint that was to guide their development. Therefore, the statement "we are God" actually has viable meaning.

The blueprint that was laid out contained many different ideas. It first held the notion that polarity and fragmentation would be the norm. The encoding in the blueprint provided the option of Free Will on the part of each fragment or soul. The challenge was in remembering that each consciousness possessed it. The more Free Will is used, the more divine memory is invoked. When faced with a polarized reality, Free Will becomes the liberator. When a soul forgets it possesses Free Will, the lessons become much more challenging, yet quite rewarding.

Another idea present in this chosen blueprint was that fragments of the Whole would be entirely responsible for their actions during this state of amnesia. Whether or not it was remembered, every action taken would generate a response from the universe. Some have called this karma; however, it is much more than "an eye for an eye." Instead of punishments for negative behavior, there is always the option of expanding one's awareness. Therefore, in a sense, wisdom "erases" karma.

Though this may sound like the rules for some kind of cruel cosmic game, the outcome has already been decided. With this in mind, it is not necessarily the destination that counts but the journey along the way. It is literally *how* the game is played.

Another blueprint agreed to was an etherically generated code built into the fabric of the universal tapestry. This code would allow bipedal, carbon-based humanoid forms to be the normal, naturally developing vehicle for the incarnation of human-type consciousness on planetary structures. This code exists on meta-atomic levels that science is just beginning to learn to measure. The symbology of polarity plays out in the human body form. The Earth human is symmetrical, with two arms, two legs, two eyes, ears, etc. The body is joined into a whole by a torso and a head.

It was also decided that during the evolutionary development of humanoid forms (within the Earth's galactic family) that the male and female polarities would manifest in separate but complimentary body types. This serves as a reminder that in order to create, polarities must always be joined or integrated. The notion is widely held that an individual has a tendency to feel most "at One" when he/she is joined with another in love.

What was the actual process of the Dimensional Infusion? There exists within the time/space fabric of the constellation Lyra what can be called a white hole.[1] Compare this white hole to a prism. In passing a beam of light through a prism, one gets a spectrum of light fragmented into seven visible color frequencies. When a portion of the Whole passed through the *Prism of Lyra* (the white hole), consciousness was fragmented into seven vibratory frequencies that represent the mass consciousness of Earth's galactic family. Each fragment became conscious on all of these different frequencies or densities. Frequencies were previously experienced as being integrated into the Whole (like white light). When this portion of the Whole passed through the prism, it manifested as seven aware frequencies. Consciousness also fragmented, and the fragments moved "away" from each other as the "Big Bang" theory symbolically suggests. The illusion thus arose that each fragment was very, very alone.

The Whole understood that the purpose of this experience was to learn to reintegrate from a point of separation. But how? As individual souls or in groups the fragments sought out the universe that was just created. The Dimensional Infusion not only created a consciousness fragmentation, but it also created the stars, planets, gases, and molecules that make up physical reality. However, physical reality represents only a few of the energy frequencies that emerged from the fragmentation.

As science has discovered, matter is densified energy vibrating at a specific rate. Every aspect of the universe is made up of energy. In Earth technology it has not yet been discovered how to measure certain portions of reality. If technology possessed this ability, an infinite

---

1   A white hole is a focus of intense light and energy. In this case, it is a birthplace.

number of gateways into time, space and dimension would be seen. For the time being, the seven frequency levels that Earth's galactic family fragmented into by passing through the Prism of Lyra will be explored below. From this point forward the term "density" will be used in reference to these frequency levels.[2]

First Density: Awareness as a point; Physical matter.

This frequency level is the most basic. It provides the matter and energy for the creation of atoms and molecules. The basic life forms of mineral and water, for example, are all operating from first-density frequency. Humans possess this frequency within themselves as well. It makes up the basic genetic codes.

Second Density: Awareness as a line; Biological matter; Development of group or species identity.

The consciousness expressed by second-density vibration does not possess self-awareness (or ego). Most species within the plant and animal kingdoms exist here; however, their placement in density depends upon many additional factors, including the presence or absence of ego.

Third Density: Volumetric awareness; Ego; Loss of group identity, development of individual identity; Ability to remember past and cognize the future while retaining present awareness.

This is the density where human beings emerge. It is a vibration that creates the illusion of separation and thus a challenge toward awakening. Presently humanity is going through a transition period into fourth-density reality which can account for the many rapid changes the human race is undergoing. This is the frequency that expresses the most separation from the Whole. It is from here that many lessons about integration are learned. This is the most intense of all levels in its cultivation of growth within the Self.

Cetaceans (dolphins and whales) presently exist simultaneously in third and fourth densities and are transitioning out of third along with humanity. The consciousness of primates exists in third density as

---

2   See the Glossary of Terms for the differences between "density" and "dimension." The difference is subtle but important.

well. The evolution of primates is becoming increasingly apparent, as one begins to observe them displaying several characteristics that were once thought of as indigenous only to humans (such as language acquisition and pathological behavior).

Fourth Density: Containment of volumetric awareness; Superconsciousness; Reintegration of group identity without loss of ego identity; As vibration increases, perception of past, present, and future become more fluid along with the ability to interface with multidimensional and multidensity realities; Negatively oriented consciousness becomes more difficult to maintain.

Presently on Earth, fourth-density reality is overlapping third. In humanity's case, this can account for the increased desire for unity, peace, and unconditional love as opposed to the illusion of separation that characterizes third density. The vibratory rate of one's reality is stepped up, and therefore one may be faced with personal issues in a much more rapid and intense way. It is easy to see how this is coming into play with the thousands of individuals upon Earth who are in therapy, in substance-abuse programs, and engaging in humanistic efforts to better the planet. This is the frequency of responsibility. This is the frequency when one begins to remember the encoding of Free Will. This is the last frequency where physical bodies are the vehicles for the expression of consciousness. Hence many civilizations choose to spend long periods of time within this density.

Fifth Density: Experiential awareness of "I" as a group identity; Not bound by linear time.

In this density sentient consciousness begin to awaken to its heritage. This is the density of wisdom. As one awakens the wisdom within, they very often want to share it with those who are still focused in the lower densities. Many from this realm choose to become guides for others. A fifth-density being merges with its family of consciousness ("oversoul" or "higher self," if you will) and begins to remember. This is the first density in which a nonphysical orientation is experienced.

(Note: There is no clear-cut distinction when transitioning from fifth to sixth and sixth to seventh densities. Because these densities are not physically oriented, there is much blending in these transitions.)

Sixth Density: Awareness as the dimension itself.

This has often been called the "Christ Consciousness" in that it displays a frequency level equal to that of the Christ or Buddha. From this frequency a total remembrance occurs, and one begins taking responsibility for the Whole rather than the Self. The process of progressing the Self and progressing the Whole become one and the same.

Seventh Density: Awareness as the multidimensional experience; Group-matrix identity (Social Memory Complex).

This is the frequency of total oneness or integration. Those who vibrate to this frequency are merged in identity and become a mass-conscious whole. They magnetize those in other frequencies and provide the current for the natural flow toward integration. Once the seventh density beings reach critical mass, they will progress through the Prism of Lyra (from our point of view it will then be a black-hole exit point) and reach the next octave, where another adventure awaits.

It is important to note that as portions of the Whole fragmented through the Prism of Lyra, each consciousness retained awareness on *all* density levels. However, part of the forgetfulness remained. From most highly focused density levels (such as third and portions of fourth), an unawareness may occur concerning the coexistence of other levels. As integration occurs, one becomes aware of these other aspects.

The microcosm always reflects the macrocosm. This is visible in the "coincidence" of how atomic structure mirrors the structure of a solar system. It is the same with the fragmentation of portions of the Whole into individual beings or soul groups. When one incarnates into a physical body, it can be likened to a mini-passage through the Prism of Lyra.

The process of soul fragmentation as one incarnates physically can be likened somewhat to Freud's id, ego, and superego theories. As a fetus, the soul demonstrates a first-density consciousness. At that point, one is aware of itself as intricately connected to the environment. Physically, one is a mass of DNA codes with the potential to become a conscious human being. Since Freud did not take his hypothesis into prenatal development, there is no correlation. If he were to have created a label that described the fetus' relationship to its environment, then it would have been a first-density description.

When the child is between birth and two years old, he/she begins to demonstrate second-density consciousness. A separation begins to be perceived between itself and the environment and its desires become externalized. There is still somewhat of an egocentric point of view, which correlates this developmental level with the id. What distinguishes a child's second-density orientation from third density is the lack of a distinct ability to differentiate between itself and the environment.

From approximately the second year of life onward, third-density consciousness becomes the primary framework demonstrated. This is the development of the ego and the awareness of the child as a separate individual. These are crucial formative years; one can see that if development is disrupted (such as through abuse) the personality can fragment and perhaps create dysfunction later in life. Many individuals retain this third-density consciousness orientation of ego throughout their entire lives.

The development of the superego, or higher awareness, is a typical fourth-density trait. Humans have the option to develop this aspect of themselves. This is a reintegration of the fragmentation of personality that occurs through the birth process, as well as integration on a spiritual level. As the human race begins to move more solidly into fourth-density consciousness, it is suspected that this personality fragmentation process will become less apparent, and perhaps children will begin displaying fourth-density characteristics earlier in their development and retain them throughout their lives.

In childhood one must learn how to adapt and integrate into a workable framework. If one cannot do this (such as in the instance of child abuse) psychological disorders will very often be displayed when adulthood is reached. Pathologies such as Multiple Personality Disorder can occur because the natural third-density personality integration process did not occur during childhood. Some extraterrestrial civilizations have learned to detect and transmute the seeds of pathological disorders during childhood, and therefore have no incidence of adult pathologies.

If it is understood that no matter how far an individual fragments (either on a soul level or in the personality), and that the way back home is always through integration, he/she will never lose sight of the goal. In this case, we can go home again.

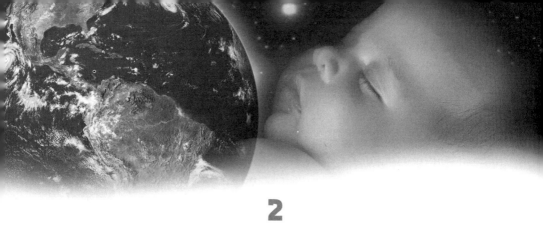

2

Creation of the Galactic Family

I am Ra, from whom time began.
I am the hub of a wheel,
A day star hovering over an endless sea.
I am not the harvest; I am the seed.
I am not the Lyre; I am the song.
I will not pass away.

—*Egyptian Book of the Dead*, Ellis Translation

In passing through the Prism of Lyra, the first fragmentation created a group of beings that can be called the Founders.[1] The Founders embodied the group consciousness of what eventually became humankind. They can project to a very high level of fourth density, but their natural state is nonphysical. In splitting off from the portion of the Whole that passed through the Prism of Lyra, they still retained a memory, if somewhat dreamlike, of the idea of integration and the purpose of the fragmentation. It is they who orchestrate humankind's evolution. They play the roles of the parent archetype, in male and female polarity balance.

The Founders became aware of the blueprint that was chosen as they fragmented from the Whole. From this blueprint they knew that

---

1   Terms such as the Watchers, the Eternals, the Reflectors, and the Seeders (among others) have been used by people to refer to these ancient beings, and are equally appropriate.

"children" carry the encodings of the "parents." Since they played the parents' role, it was their responsibility to influence the growth of the new consciousness about to be created. In doing this they *became* the blueprint, began to understand and live it, knowing that this would encode future fragments.

The Founders began to understand the natural energy patterns of the polarized reality just created. It became obvious to them that the newly fragmented group consciousness interfaces with specific realities (i.e. densities) within three main points: (1) A point of pure positivity; (2) A point of pure negativity; (3) The integrative point of the two. All interactions occur within the lines that connect each point, with very few aspects of consciousness existing within the points of purity. This realization inspired them to understand a paradigm of polarized reality, which was something exciting and new to their understanding. The paradigm, as it emerged for them, is shown below in a two-dimensional diagram.

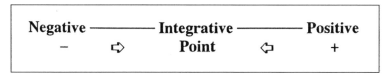

Both negative and positive polarities moving toward integration.

As they pondered the paradigm they began to understand the mechanics of how the fragmented consciousness would once again merge back through the Prism of Lyra. The linear model above can be changed to bring about the triadic relationship of the template. Here is an illustration:

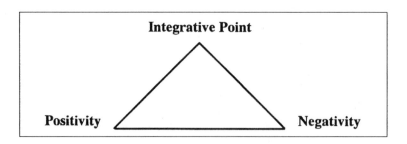

This triad represents the probabilities of the integrative process. Civilizations naturally move randomly (according to the laws of chaos) within the triadic template until a balance of energy is reached.

If a civilization or consciousness chooses integration (the willingness to grow from both polarities), they will naturally move toward the integrative point, fueled by the momentum of both polarities. This can be viewed as an allowing form of integration. If, on the other hand, a civilization or individual refuses integration, the template expands to accommodate their denial of the opposite polarity. The expanded template will not be outlined here at the present time.

When they believed they were ready, the Founders began another fragmentation. Just as a portion of the Whole became curious and created this realm from its thoughts, the Founders emulated their "parents" and exerted thought energy to create a fragmentation of themselves. This fragmentation occurred far and wide; individualized consciousness sprang from the Founders' group awareness and began to explore the universe. Because of this fragmentation, every being existing in the galactic family presented here is part of the Founders.

There are an infinite number of fragments and explorational journeys. Some of these fragments grew into civilizations that have played a part in the development of Earth. Some of those who have a reference point in Earth's known reality will be explored in the chapters ahead.

When the Founders fragmented, some allowed their energy to densify sufficiently in order to enter a physical reality. The Founders had already chosen planets that could support humanoid life. Then they gently guided these fragments into a physical, third- or fourth-density existence. After time had passed, the fragments became more accustomed to physical existence, and assistance from the Founders (who still existed in smaller numbers) became less needed.

The first area to be eventually colonized after the Founders' fragmentation was in the general vicinity of the Lyra constellation. Most of the galactic family that has genetic connections to Earth has roots in the Lyran system. It was there that the first attempt at integration occurred. The Founders thought that it would be easy and predictable; instead, humanoid life forms spread outward exponentially until a very intricate tapestry was woven. The threads of the tapestry began to become tangled until eventually the origins of the thread became lost in the colorful maze of the tapestry's design.

The following are the main characters displayed in this tapestry from the perspective of Earth:

LYRA

The general area of the "birth" of the humanoid race. All humanoid races in our galactic family have genetic roots connected to Lyra. It is the symbolic harp upon which the song of humanity is played.

VEGA

A star within the constellation of Lyra. Descendants of Lyra, Vega birthed a race of beings who manifested Lyra's opposite polarity both in their beliefs and actions. There were frequent conflicts between the Lyran and Vegan races.

APEX PLANET

A planet within the Lyran system which was the first attempt at creating an integrated society.

SIRIUS

A trinary star group, it is known in Earth mythology as the Dog Star. Sirius was one of the first areas to be colonized by beings from the Lyran star group. Sirius embodied the energy of the triadic template and perpetuated the drive toward integration. There is a large variety of consciousness types that incarnate in this system.

ORION

This is the main "battleground" for the challenge of polarity integration, seeded from Sirius as well as Lyra and Vega. There is a direct connection with Earth, as explored in later chapters.

PLEIADES

Colonized by Lyran offshoots, this group is Earth's main genetic connection from extraterrestrial sources.

ARCTURUS

An archetype or future-self ideal of Earth, Arcturus assists in healing personal and planetary consciousness. Its vibration, primarily sixth density, has been attributed to the angelic kingdom.

ZETA RETICULI

This civilization is intimately connected with Earth. The Reticuli are the primary group instigating abductions (or more accurately called "temporary detainments" since this group always returns the abductee). More will be said about this group in later chapters.

Though some of these civilizations overlap each other in time and may not appear linear, below is a linear translation of the progression of various cultures in comparison to each other.

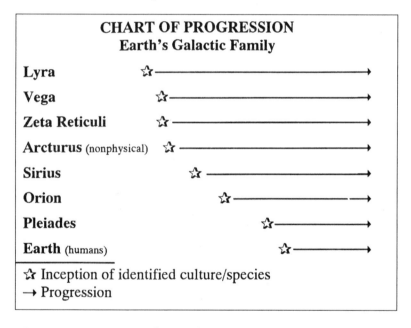

Once one recovers from the initial shock of the idea that extraterrestrials had something to do with Earth's heritage, it really seems like a very logical explanation. Why would the human race egotistically believe that it alone is responsible for Earth's genetic past? Upon Earth, races have "discovered" new races and have begun integrating with them. Perhaps before this occurred, these races never knew the others existed. This model can hold true for the universe as well as planet Earth. How many more ancient drawings of rocketships and their pilots need to be found before humans can break through the fears about discovering Earth's past?

The most obvious question is this: If the extraterrestrials are out there, why don't they show themselves? An answer can be found in humanity's approach to anthropological studies upon Earth. Scientists do not go marching right in to a "primitive" culture waving their cameras and equipment. These types of cultural assimilations sometimes take them decades to accomplish. In its own eyes, humanity may seem "civilized" enough. However, to a race that has achieved space travel and perhaps even global unity, humanity may seem primitive indeed. Perhaps they are waiting, hiding in the bushes, allowing only a few humans to see them until the signal goes out to the whole of society that they are not a threat.

What if the signal that they are there never goes out to society? What if humanity continues to ignore the evidence, hoping it will all go away? To many of the extraterrestrials, this seems to be the case. All nonthreatening methods seem to have been unsuccessful thus far. The primary game plan over the last many decades appears to be much more profound in its potential to awaken humanity. Some of Earth's visitors are now using fear. At times society is so quick to validate negativity rather than positivity that humanity's own framework may now begin to be used to assimilate Earth to its previously denied reality. Fear awakens—rather rudely at that. Perhaps that explains the growing observation of extraterrestrial abduction experiences as a method of awakening humanity to a greater reality.

At humanity's level of development, a model for the natural evolution of a planet has not yet been formulated. It seems obvious that a civilization would not be able to reach the cosmos and the folding of space-time dimensions if it cannot resolve its conflicts on a planetary level. The expansion of consciousness required for such a leap may be dependent upon the unified whole. If the whole is not integrated and balanced, attempts may be fruitless. Humanity may be experiencing this limitation now, with so many unsuccessful space-launch attempts as well as space program budget restrictions. Earth may just not be ready. Humanity wants to reach for the stars but very often cannot even reach for the hand of its neighbor.

The extraterrestrial connection is important, but what is even more important is developing a global perspective. Expansion will come from action—the claiming of responsibility for Earth by humanity itself. The extraterrestrials will not intervene to clean up humanity's mess. Earth is entering adulthood and has been kicked out of the nest. It would serve humanity to release its victimhood, claim its divine birthright, and create heaven on Earth. The extraterrestrials can only remind humanity of its unlimited potential. Their communication (and our awareness of Earth's heritage) can be likened to a dangling carrot. If the human race wants that carrot, perhaps it must do what needs to be done to get it—unify and integrate.

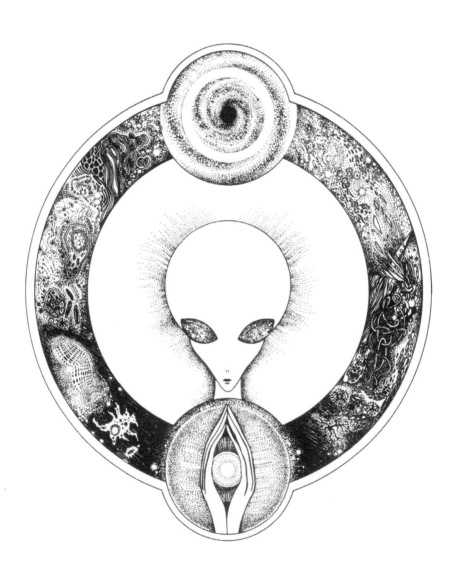

3

The Womb of Lyra

"When I became," said he,
"the becoming became.
I have become the becoming.
I am one seeing myself, divided.
I am two and four and eight.
I am the universe in diversity.
I am my transformations.
This is my coming together.
Here are my selves become one."

—*Egyptian Book of the Dead*, Ellis Translation

From the point of view of a reality that can be perceived by physical beings, the form of the Founders has two arms, two legs, a head, and a torso. They possess large, inquisitive eyes as a symbolic representation of their desire for knowledge and of the ancient memory they carry within them. Physical beings would view them as insectlike, very tall, and having long, graceful limbs. Third-density humans can perceive them if they enter an accelerated version of fourth density. Interactions with them are usually able to occur in an altered state. From this state they appear etheric and dreamlike.[1]

---

1   In dream symbology, the Founders may translate into figures like large insects such as praying mantises, walking sticks, and even grasshoppers.

Having fragmented their consciousness further, the Founders began solidifying energy into matter. This created a prototype physical race into which the majority of humanoid consciousness would incarnate. On meta-atomic levels, organizational codes exist which create a consistent humanoid-type body in a carbon-based environment as the vehicle for physical representation of consciousness.[2] The Founders used this naturally occurring code to assist them in creating versions of themselves in both physical and nonphysical states. This form symbolically reflected the aspects of the polarized universe they had entered. Again, it is representative of the idea that "parents" create "children" in their own image.

The Founders are the energetic grandparents of the human race. It was their desire to manifest different dimensional aspects of themselves. This would produce root forms of life which would facilitate the process of creating diversity within the new reality that was just born. They are both the Source and the prototype.

As they emerged into this light form through the densification of energy, they became aware that all life will once again evolve back into the Founders and then into the Source. Consciousness will scatter and fragment, sometimes beyond recognition; but it will evolve back into the Source physically, as well as mentally, emotionally, and spiritually.

Thus the Founders began the next step of the fragmentation process. Their first action was to begin making the plans necessary to spread life throughout the Lyran system. They were aware that over time the life forms would naturally gravitate into planetary civilizations by means of attraction.

Planets were chosen within the Lyran star group to house these new races. As these planets naturally began to develop primate life, the Founders seeded these developing primates with plasmic energy[3] on meta-atomic levels within their DNA structure. This occurred over many generations until the primates/humanoids possessed the genetics necessary to sustain the higher vibrations of third-density consciousness. With slight alterations, the incarnation process was soon to begin on several planetary bodies.

---

2   This idea is reflected in Rupert Sheldrake's work with morphic resonance, which shows there are energetic fields that organize all form. These fields can pass on characteristics to "unrelated" aspects of the same species that are not necessarily in physical proximity to each other.

3   Highly condensed energy manifesting as light or liquid light.

The Founders fragmented themselves further in order to release the consciousness necessary to incarnate on these planets. As this fragmentation occurred, each consciousness was magnetized to a specific planet where the vibrations were more compatible with the individual fragment.

As expressed in the previous chapter, the basic template of the consciousness that fragmented through the Prism of Lyra can be considered a triad. It represents one polarity, its opposite, and the integrative point. The Founders observed this natural flow of energy emerging in the base species that were developing. These different planetary groups were initially homogeneous, not yet manifesting any single aspect of the template in an obvious way.

As time went on and interactions between individuals and groups increased, many groups polarized into either negative or positive orientations.[4] Some groups began to display varying degrees of integration. This scenario was expected by the Founders. However, the process began to take on a life of its own. As the process grew exponentially, the Founders began to see the infinite reflections of the Whole, and to some extent it became overwhelming to them.

As these groups evolved and achieved space travel, they exposed themselves to the development of other planetary groups in the area. Cultures began to mix and grow. New philosophies were born. For a period of time the Lyran races rapidly developed advanced technology, expansive philosophy, and strong social development due to the interactions between these planetary cultures. Then the dynamics of the template began to be displayed.

Polarities began to solidify, generating their own polarization that continued exponentially in turn. Negative polarities began splitting and manifesting their own negative/positive poles. Positive poles did the same. The feminine expressed its masculine, and the masculine expressed its feminine. Polarities exploded like viruses within the previously blossoming civilization.

The simple set of mirrors that the Founders had created shattered into infinite fragments. They had lost direct contact with many of the genetic windows (physical beings) that they had created. The physical beings had now taken on lives of their own, although the

---

4   These negative/positive orientations are not judgments. They are representative of the idea of poles—equal but possessing opposite energy.

original programs continued to be an underlying factor influencing their development.

The first group to develop as a specific non-Lyran species was the Vegan civilization.[5] They formed a highly distinctive philosophy and spiritual orientation and began to isolate themselves from the Lyran races. They were initially a negatively-oriented civilization, expressed as the negative pole of Lyra because they had adopted a philosophy of service to self (contraction). Lyra itself may be considered the positive pole because all other civilizations were "born" out of it (expansion).

As time passed, friction grew between the people of the Lyran races and the Vegan civilizations. Neither group was progressing in an integrative way. Both possessed within themselves the conflict of polarity. Neither group was right or wrong; they all played out the same ideas, only from a different perspective. They just could not understand how to balance their energies. Polarization continued to grow exponentially as they grappled with their relationships between their civilizations and themselves.

A third civilization began to emerge from the Lyran races. Because this planet was the apex of a symbolic triangle of integration (playing out both negative and positive polarities), it can be called the Apex planet during this stage of its development. Later, it becomes a much more intricate piece of this galactic puzzle.

The Apex planet began its civilization by drawing in characteristics from both the Lyra and Vega polarities. Genetically they were a mixture. Within their race, diversity was even more widespread than upon our present Earth. There were dark- and light-skinned people, pacifists and conquerors, artists, musicians, and soldiers. Even in comparison to our Earth race, they did not coexist peacefully at all. Separation began occurring in the culture until the entire planet was engulfed in the friction of polarity. No resolution was in sight. The future of this Apex planet seemed hopeless—they eventually allowed pollution and weaponry to nearly destroy their world.

When opposite polarities are forced, not integrated, they cause fusion. This fusion manifested on the Apex world as nuclear war. A small number of inhabitants secured themselves underground, but the remainder perished from their own inability to integrate. What

5 Vega is the Alpha star (the brightest) in the Lyra constellation.

occurred on a planetary scale was quite interesting. From a point of observation in space, it appeared that the planet destroyed itself. From the point of view of the survivors who went underground, they were very much alive. As a result of their nuclear explosions their planet was eventually propelled into an alternate dimension.

After the cataclysm, radiation upon their world remained quite high which forced them to stay underground. Once they recovered from their emotional shock, it became time to pick up the shattered pieces of their lives. Their development and their amazing transformation will be explored in further chapters, for they play a vital role not only in the transformation of planet Earth but of the galactic family and the Founders as well.

Meanwhile, the Lyran races and the Vegan civilizations were continuing with their development. Groups of Lyrans wished to remove themselves from the friction with Vega and sought out many other areas to colonize. Groups of Vegans also escaped their planet's conflicts and founded a number of civilizations including Altair and Centauri (which will not be addressed in this material). Gone were the clear-cut lines of traceable philosophic and genetic history. Humanity was spreading quickly, carrying with it the seeds of experience and polarity. The goal was always buried deep within the souls of each being and it gently nudged them onward. The goal was, and still is, integration.

It is apparent that the beginnings of the entrance into polarity by the Founders was not easy. They had created an equation that they expected would conclude according to their calculations. As with the new science of chaos, the movement of energy between these three civilizations (Lyra, Vega, and Apex) became unpredictable to the Founders. The entire galactic family could only wait and watch, knowing that in chaos there is order—divine order.

These early lessons have been imprinted into humanity's etheric memory as a reminder of all that it has been and all that it can become. Humanity is never alone in this struggle. The Founders still wait silently. They exist not only "out there" but also within the soul of humanity as its most basic archetype. The cycle of life and existence is merely a circle; the beginning and end are the same. When humanity feels the call of evolution, it is the Founders whispering through the expanse of time and dimension. They are a part of humankind speaking to itself. Perhaps it is time to listen.

4

The Sirius Factor

Blazing as the star that cometh forth at Harvest-time,
Shining forth amid the host of stars
In the darkness of the night, the star whose name
Men call Orion's Dog. Brightest of all is he, yet
For an evil sign is he set, and bringeth much
Fever upon hapless men …

—*The Illiad*

The realm of Sirius was one of the first to be explored by the curious consciousness that passed through the Prism of Lyra and fragmented from the Founders. Sirius represents a very important symbol for the entire galactic family—that of the triad. Though it has not been scientifically validated by most astronomers, Sirius is a trinary star group.[1] Symbolically, this represents the template—two polarities at the base of a triangle, and the joining or integrating of the polarities at the apex. It reflects the basic foundation of the galactic family's desire—to once again unify through the merging of polarity.

After the Infusion, many consciousnesses who chose to remain nonphysical attracted themselves to the realm of Sirius. Here they

---

1   Some astronomers, such as Van Den Bos and Finsen at the Union Observatory in the 1920s and, more recently, D. Lauterborn are theorizing that Sirius is indeed a trinary star group, but no viable data has been uncovered to confirm that claim.

began laying the physical as well as nonphysical groundwork for the vital role Sirius was to play in the unfolding drama. They were to become some of the earliest genetic and etheric engineers following in the footsteps of the Founders.

Anticipating what was to come, these nonphysical Sirians began forming (through the transmutation of energy into matter) a third-density world that would eventually be able to support physical life. They also created more vibrationally focused realms for the consciousnesses that would choose to exist there in the nonphysical state. Thus, because of their ability to create realms suitable for all manifestations of consciousness, they became known as the Elders of Sirius.

During the Lyran and Vegan conflicts, representatives from both polarities inhabited the Sirius realm with the desire to integrate there. The Elders of Sirius prepared for an influx of both positive and negative energy. They were quite aware of the scenario that needed to occur.

The Vegans who chose to inhabit the Sirius realm decided to incarnate physically within a third-density reality. Culturally they were highly polarized in the masculine, and their philosophy was one of domination, which was becoming more difficult to maintain in fourth density. They felt they must dominate their environment and control their evolution. According to them, this would allow them a mastership of their realm, and from that point their evolution would then progress at an accelerated pace.

From this desire the Vegans began plans for their colonization of a planet orbiting one of the Sirius suns. If they were to maintain their philosophic orientation of domination, the natural polarization inherent in this philosophy could only be perpetuated in a third-density existence. They were to be tightly focused in the physical, creating a veil of illusion and forgetfulness even more dense than presently on Earth. They were so sure of their own abilities (and so unaware of the lure of third-density separation) that they zealously began speeding up the evolutionary process of the primate-like species developing on the world they had chosen. As soon as the DNA of the indigenous species matched their desire, they began incarnating.

Almost immediately, these new Sirians lost their memory connection with Vega. The veil was too dense. Their desire to create forgetfulness was so strong that they remembered nothing of their origin. They did not dream. They did not meditate. They did not pursue creative activities except to maintain their structure of domination. When their zealousness translated into physical reality, it created a culture driven by the desire for domination—over each other and the universe around them.

As this negative Sirian planet was developing, a group from Lyra decided to venture outward into the Sirius system. These beings chose to remain in the nonphysical realms. Their orientation was polarized toward the idea of service to others. They were particularly interested in the physical healing of those in pain. The combination of the negative Sirians (who denied their spiritual self) and the positive, nonphysical Sirians originally from Lyra (who felt it was their duty to heal all those in pain) created a dynamic of tension that echoed throughout the Sirius system and beyond.

The saga began. The positives began bombarding the negatives with love and healing energy on the subconscious and unconscious levels. Because the negatives were so tightly focused, this created psychological pain for them. The more the negatives resisted, the more the positives sent healing energy. Friction occurred from this interaction that was very uncomfortable for all consciousness in the Sirius system. The Elders of Sirius finally intervened.

It was decided that the conflict would once again be moved to another locale. This time integration would be attempted from a slightly less polarized perspective. The Elders sought out a home for this conflict. It did not take them long to discover the electromagnetic properties of the area called Orion. Thus the myth begins of how Sirius, the Dog Star, leads the way for the Hunter—Orion.

Once the initial conflict was removed from the Sirius system, the physical civilization remained. They had cut themselves off from spirit even to the point of death, where an immediate reincarnation into the system occurred again, further alienating them from any form of nonphysical existence. Therefore, most of the negative society was unaware of a conflict, so they could not be made aware of its movement into the Orion system. Their society continued within its haze of forgetfulness. Those desiring the negative/positive integration now went to Orion from Lyra/Vega instead of to Sirius. Sometimes, very infrequently, a soul would awaken from the negative Sirius world and progress to the Orion arena.

From the positive (nonphysical) Sirius perspective, they would now be able to directly influence the ailing negatives. Many joyously ventured to Orion to carry out this task. Others chose to remain within the Sirius realm, concentrating their healing abilities toward other goals. Other positives from Lyra joined the Orion struggle. Galactic history was born.

Because of the positive Sirians' desire to facilitate physical healing (their service to physicality instead of choosing incarnation), they allied themselves with the energies of Arcturus. Arcturus is oriented toward the idea of emotional healing. Together they form the Sirius/Arcturus Matrix. This matrix has found its way onto nearly every physical planet within the galactic family as a holistic energy representing the healing of body, mind, and spirit.

Planet Earth has known the Sirius/Arcturus Matrix in many forms. It is an archetypal energy that is used by an individual or society for many purposes. It is malleable and can be shaped into any appropriate definition. Whatever the shape, it is devoted to the service of physicality. The Sirius/Arcturus Matrix reminds the fragments of their connection to the Whole and their natural abilities for self-healing.

Though it is only a small percentage, a group of positive Sirians decided to incarnate into physicality as well. However, they rejected the humanoid form for a form that is more representative of their nature. This form is the cetacean. Dolphins and whales represent a translation of Sirius energy upon a physical, polarized world. In archetypal symbology, water represents the subconscious. Cetaceans are there silently—in Earth's oceans and in the sea of humanity's subconscious. They remain as a reminder of humanity's potential for integration.

Of all the energies that are a part of the immediate galactic family, the Sirius energy is the most widely used upon Earth. The name Sirius means "The Sparkling One" or "The Scorching One," also called the "The Dog Star" and the "The Nile Star." Perhaps because it is the brightest and the second nearest star visible to Earth (8.7 light-yearss away), many ancient cultures recognized the importance of the Sirius energy, most notably the Egyptians.

At times, Sirius consciousness may choose to densify its frequency to become visible to third-density humans. During many of the Egyptian dynasties it was quite common to have a visitation from a

Sirian in the disguise of one of their gods (such as Isis, Osiris, and Anubis). These "costumes" made it easier for the Egyptians to honor their presence, and often the visitations triggered memories of the very early days when the "gods" walked openly upon Earth. These Sirians gave the Egyptians (as well as other Earth cultures) much advanced astronomical and medical information. Even today, scholars are still questioning the origin of this information.

Halfway across the globe, the Mayan culture had its own unique relationship with Sirius. Advanced medical practices and galactic astronomical information were imparted to them that presently have not been unraveled by modern scholars. Theirs was a much more personal relationship with Sirius. These Mayans were, in a sense, tourists from the Sirius realm (incarnate here on Earth) who wanted to experience physicality from a closer vantage point. Their relationship with the Mayans was so intimate that the Sirians actually shared with them the technology of transmutation—from matter to pure energy/consciousness. When their lessons were complete, the masters of the Mayan race vanished (transmuted), leaving behind a trail for humanity to follow.

These Sirians left behind many time capsules and puzzles for future generations to discover. One of these puzzles is the crystal skull.

The crystal skull can represent the infinite nature of man and consciousness. Looking into its depths, one can sense the past and future. Humans have not yet learned how to translate the data and emotions that are triggered when one gazes into its expanse. Perhaps one day information encoded within the skull may ignite sparks of memory within humanity, as the Sirians have possibly intended. They are one of the primary groups who, in many forms, have left the clues about Earth's past.

It is important to note that the Sirians are not meant to be spoken about as a group of extraterrestrials as much as a group consciousness expressing itself both physically and nonphysically. They have been a guiding force for the developing civilization upon Earth. As will be explored in later chapters, they are one of the primary characters in the creation of the human species on Earth.

Returning now to the negative Sirius planet, Earth has an analogous translation of its philosophy. The practice that is called "black magic" or the "dark arts" is rooted in the philosophy of the negative Sirians. Within the Egyptian culture the organized worship of the negative force took place within the temples and priesthoods of Set. This philosophy rejects the idea of reinclusion into the universal fabric. Those that practice this philosophy consider themselves unique, separate, and egocentric. The illusion that they have created is one of nonresponsibility for their actions. It often takes them many lessons and sometimes many lifetimes to recognize that their actions and their beliefs create the very reality from which they are trying to escape.

In translation, another manifestation of the Sirius influence on Earth from a slightly negative perspective is the Illuminati. The Illuminati are a group of physical and nonphysical negatively oriented (and even some positively oriented) extraterrestrials who came to Earth as physical beings during the Inception.[2]

These beings eventually felt they did not get the recognition (or power) they thought they deserved.[3] Many of these early off-planet consciousnesses who interacted with humanity had allowed their energies or their "histories" to evolve and become an archetype to assist Earth. The idea of control is their identity. If they cannot control others, they feel as if they do not exist...and they are terrified of nonexistence. This motivation has caused them to attempt to interfere in Earth's development from the start. As with an annoying insect, they are a bother, but rarely cause serious problems. Only the individuals who have no sense of their own power will be found in those power structures upon Earth that stem from fear of powerlessness. They cannot be an influence if one does not allow them to be. It all comes back to the issue of claiming one's own power.

One final idea concerning contemporary manifestations of the Sirius energy has to do with the appearance of menacing extraterrestrials as seen in UFO literature. For the most part, severely negative UFO experiences, cattle mutilations, and the "Men in Black" phenomenon are connected to the negative Sirius (and Orion) group who actually generate more fear than damage. At times the physical Sirians (and

2   The Illuminati are not only comprised of Sirians. Other groups, such as Orion, are part of the Illuminati structure.
3   These beings represent only a small percentage of Sirius consciousness. Since the Earth Inception the planet has developed some very strong positive relationships with Sirius beings who have been some of the main supporters of humanity.

Orions) can break through the layers of protection in the solar system and try to wreak havoc. What is their motivation?

In exploring the ancient Sumerian texts concerning early history and the nature of the conflicts of the gods, one gets a clear idea that Earth (in whole or in part) was involved with issues of territorial dispute by various groups at different times. The question has often been asked why the Sirians seem to be so involved in Earth's development. If it is indeed true that Sirius is a trinary star group (as the Dogon tribe's astronomical traditions suggest), could it be that Sol (Earth's sun) is or once was the third star? If that is the case, Earth may have been part of a territorial dispute among the Sirians from its very inception. This could explain why the negative Sirians consider it to be their right to do as they wish on Earth and why they point an accusing finger at other extraterrestrials for wrongly interfering with Sirian internal affairs, thus creating many historical disputes. The Sirians may consider Earth to be part of their territory. In present time, Sol is only 8.7 light-years away from the Sirius system which has been considered by astronomers to be part of our local star family.

Many of the early Sirians were quite adept at genetic engineering. During the Earth Inception the physical Sirians placed a latent DNA code within the early humans. When Earth beings reach a certain vibratory frequency as a race, this code will be triggered. This code will assist those on Earth in remembering humanity's galactic past. Contemporary negative Sirians are terrified of this. They have continually kept themselves from transitioning into fourth density for fear of nonexistence. They fear that if Earth transitions, they will transition also and cease to exist. They believe if they keep society in fear, Earth will not be able to make the shift. As a whole, they cannot determine humanity's fate, for Earth humans have more power than the negative Sirians realize. But they will continue. They know no other way.

Whether dealing with physical extraterrestrials or archetypal energy, the Sirian identity is entwined with humanity's. It is rich with knowledge as well as challenge. One must always remember Sirius as the triad and what it represents—integration of polarity—which is the destiny of Earth.

5

The Winds of Orion

Begirt with many a blazing star,
Stood the great giant Algebar,
Orion, hunter of the beast!
His sword hung gleaming by his side,
And on his arm, the lion's hide
Scattered across the midnight air
The Golden Radiance of its hair …

—*Longfellow*

Canst thou bind the sweet influence of the Pleiades,
or loose the bands of Orion?

—*Job 38:31*

When two opposite polarities meet, they are naturally attracted. When they attempt fusion (rather than integration) they produce a force of enormous energy. They produce sparks. They produce change. Sometimes they even produce pain.

This was the case with the civilizations of Lyra that attempted integration within the Vegan and Sirius star systems. The conflict began playing out there, but was energetically expanded to include Orion. Its beginnings were as a Lyran conflict. Through generations it evolved into a new race's war, that of the Orions. As generations passed, each side lost touch with what they were fighting for. Yet the anguish continued.

The stakes were clearly marked. The "negative" side perpetuated the idea of service to self. Within their philosophy, if one served the self the whole was served. What they did not realize was that they were *denying* the whole by the way they chose to carry out this philosophy. This translated as the need for domination.

These were dark times indeed. Domination entailed behavior that Earth humans have never experienced. Genetic manipulation of blood lines was common, in an attempt to dilute or concentrate power. What humans know as black magic was a common practice. Beings were so saturated with their own fear that they struck out at all who were different. The Earth legends of sword and sorcery are dim remembrances carried in the etheric cell memory from the dark times of Orion.

The "positive" side epitomized the idea of service to others. It was their belief that the only way to survive was to be subservient, even at the expense of the self. So an interesting dynamic was played out. There were those individuals who were the dominators and those who were all too willing to play the victim role. These "positives" felt that to support the whole they must serve the whole and relinquish the self. In reality they were denying themselves as being a valid portion of that whole.

The Orion civilization was one of the very few that evolved into a state of technological advancement while still being in a state of intense spiritual conflict. Eons of time passed while the drama continued playing out. It began with basic emotional manipulation all the way to the other end of the spectrum—manipulation using highly advanced technological tools. Reincarnationally speaking, the same souls incarnated time and again, switching sides, trying to find a way to bring the whole struggle into balance.

Within Orion history there has always been underground resistance. Throughout the ages its strength ebbed and flowed like the pulses of their red giant Betelgeuse. Usually they would be discovered by the "negatives," disbanded, and punished. Any time they built up some momentum, it radiated too loudly and they were found.

As the philosophy of the resistance solidified, it became apparent that they needed to squelch the radiation of their ideas. They decided instead to symbolically absorb. They allowed people to come to *them*. They became like a black hole which was unable to be seen, but the force and momentum of their energy was as powerful as a silent wind. Their organization was thus called "The Black League." The symbol of their struggle became the black dragon. A new aspect of the drama began to unfold.

Now there were three facets to the struggle: There were the dominators, the victims, and the resistance (fueled by the friction of two polarities). The Black League became quite successful in thwarting the efforts of the dominators (known as the Orion Empire); however, it was only enough to reduce their momentum to a standstill. An energy impasse was reached.

Within the souls of these repressed people existed a great desperation. They knew the extent of the Orion Empire's control. The Empire had devised ways to control astral bodies; death was no longer freedom. Many individuals studied with heretic teachers to learn the ancient knowledge of dimensional consciousness travel. Few were successful, but those who were found a way out of the Orion system forever. Through focused concentration and disengagement from the Orion mass-conscious belief systems, a small percentage of individuals were able to leave their bodies (die) and successfully target or home in on beings who had escaped or were reincarnated on Earth from Orion.[1] Once these beings were targeted, the Orion entity was able to create a window through which he/she could travel. When he/she came through that window and incarnated on Earth, that being became "lost" in the Earth mass consciousness. This was a safety mechanism; if they did not know their own identity, they could not be pursued by the Orion Empire.

The escapees then entered Earth's reincarnational cycle and most likely continued to play out the Orion drama unconsciously within their soul patterns. At times they could have been immediately pursued through the window by Orion Empire representatives. Often these Empire representatives became "caught" in Earth's mass consciousness as well and had to enter the reincarnational cycle; when they incarnated they carried their old Orion desire for control with them.

---

1   The Orions had the capability to target Earth people in Earth's past, present, and future.

As the desperation grew, the Black League decided to fight even harder. They had people who played both sides. Smuggled reports from informants resulted in an even more intense resistance effort. They began to employ tactics borrowed from the dominators. All this was done in the name of freedom. They eventually learned that freedom was elusive, and the conflict intensified.

With all of their efforts the Black League could not understand why they were not being successful in liberating the victims. They became discouraged. The people hungered for a form of spirituality, but all that was present was a gnawing emptiness and fear. Nothing worked. For a few generations the Black League remained stagnant, only an idea and nothing more.

Then something miraculous occurred. During generations of spiritual gestation a seed began to grow. A soul incarnated who embodied all the hopes and dreams of the Orion races and had none of the hatred or fear. When he was born, he was safely contained in an energetically and emotionally neutral environment deep within the planet so he would not become polarized. At adulthood he began to teach. What he taught began to shed new light on the struggle. What he proposed could end it once and for all.

He taught universal laws—integration cannot be achieved through negativity. The Black League was fighting fire with fire, only creating a blaze instead of peace. One must integrate positivity and negativity to the balance point. One must *love*, not fear. The idea of peace and freedom must be loved so much that one is willing to *live* it in one's soul despite outside manifestations. The Black League thus learned that their intentions were good, but their actions only caused more of what they despised.

This realization occurred on mass levels. It opened new doors of spirituality for the people of these oppressed worlds. They had a long way to go, but at least they now knew where to start.

Once the dynamic began to be understood from higher levels, it was decided that they would transmute this energy by moving outward into the galaxy and starting fresh. From these higher levels they called upon the Founders to assist them in choosing a world. Of primary concern was an assurance that all the tools were provided on this new world for these adventurous beings to begin transmutation of the Orion energy. Free Will/Choice (rather than the control dramas of Orion) was the primary tool, as well as a latent DNA code that would trigger a desire for societal preservation when/if it became possible for them to self-destruct. The world that was chosen was Earth. The Founders then began engaging various physical groups to carry out the Earth Inception. [See chapter 9.]

Earth has manifested the Orion drama in an attempt to balance polarity throughout humankind's history. The fall of Atlantis, the Roman Empire, and the ongoing religious wars are all examples of memory patterns from Orion that are emerging to be cleared. Throughout all of these dramas the human race has survived and has kept total oppression at bay. Humanity continues to play out the same dynamic: victims, perpetrators, and resistance. However, this time light is beginning to spread and even the resistance is beginning to learn early on that one can't fight fire with fire.

The contemporary Orion civilization, existing in the same time continuum as present-day Earth, has already healed its conflict. Because Earth is still playing out Orion's past in an attempt to balance it for itself, the primary contact humanity receives from Orion has been judged to be negative. The Men in Black phenomenon as well as some manifestations of the Illuminati structure are playing out the past Orion need for control.

The Men in Black (MIBs) have several origins. Some are human incarnations from Orion and/or negatively oriented Sirius energy; others are actual past Orions who have traveled "forward" in time to present-day Earth. (These include Empire representatives who were caught in Earth's mass consciousness as they pursued Orion escapees.) They perceive Earth as a threat. From their point of view, as humanity awakens and liberates itself it magnetizes the oppressed Orion beings to seek freedom here. They want to keep these windows of opportunity closed for the victims of Orion, keep Earth unempowered, and stay in total control. The MIBs are only one manifestation of this idea; generally it is played out on Earth in a much more subtle way. Those individuals who carry the oppressive patterns from Orion act from their soul memory and are not necessarily conscious in their desire for absolute control. In researching twentieth-century MIB encounters, one comes across the ironic behavior of these beings—they function at a very autonomous level and seem to never claim for themselves the power that they so single-mindedly attempt to wrest from humans. This may suggest that the MIB is only a pawn in perhaps an even more bizarre power struggle.

The Orion drama is not an experiment done *to* someone *by* someone else. All those who choose to be a part of the Earth Transmutation do so through their Free Will. This transmutation or integration will affect the entire galactic family created through the Dimensional Infusion. This would initiate the beginning processes of the integration back through the Prism of Lyra. The integrated polarities can thus be termed the "Orion Light."

There were stages built into the Transmutation project from which the Founders would be able to gauge its progress. The first stage was a simple seeding and developing of third-density life into a strong genetic strain on Earth. The subsequent stages involved various developments of civilization. The crucial stage is occurring presently upon the Earth—the mass reawakening of millions of souls to a greater spiritual purpose.

This awakening occurs naturally and begins to accelerate a widening of the gap between the positive and negative poles (as seen presently within society). The accentuation of this gap serves to polarize and highlight the choices society may take—making it clear that choices *must* be made at this point in time. Humanity does not have the ugliness and pain of a tormented past to the extent that the Orions had. As Earth reawakens, all the tools become visible for humanity to claim responsibility for the Whole and the Self. The painful Orion memories may continue to surface, but the healing of them will occur through humanity's proclamation of freedom and liberation.

When the Dimensional Infusion occurred, there were some individual and group consciousnesses who chose to remain dormant. They allowed themselves to serve as archetypes, and could be awakened as needed. Some even allowed fragments of themselves to incarnate. An example of this is the consciousness known as Merlin. During the time of the Orion drama the friction between the two polarities awakened the sleeping magician. "He" became a guiding force in the drive to integrate from both a physical and a nonphysical point of view. Fragments of his consciousness would incarnate intermittently to spark a memory of the past and a vision of the future. He has gone by many names on many worlds, but he always mirrors one's own beauty as well as one's ugliness. His energy has been present in association with Earth right from the Inception.

The Earth Inception will be examined more thoroughly in the coming chapters. For the time being, it must be shared that this drama has been created to be a success. Most who incarnate upon Earth are involved (to varying degrees) in the Orion drama. Everyone is here by choice. The instant that one begins operating from a belief that humanity is here against its will is the instant that personal and planetary power has been surrendered.

6

Earth's Pleiadian Cousins

Many a night from yonder ivied casement
ere I went to rest,
Did I look upon great Orion,
sloping slowly to the west.
Many a night I saw the Pleiads,
rising thro' the mellow shade
Glitter like a swarm of fireflies
tangled in a silver braid.

——Tennyson

During the early development of the Lyran system the first friction between polarities began to occur. Some Lyrans manifested the idea of the feminine polarity—intuitive and allowing. They believed the path to reintegration was through inner development. Other Lyrans, however, polarized to the masculine. Their philosophy upheld the notion that in order to evolve, they had to dominate the known universe. This caused much dissension between the two.

As the Lyran civilization developed, a group of Lyrans decided they would prefer to develop their culture away from what they perceived were negative influences. Thus they searched the galaxy for a new home. In their search they found a young planet rich in natural resources. This planet was Earth.

For several generations this group resided on Earth, coexisting peacefully with the developing primate race. However, over a long period of time they found that they were not adapting to Earth's physical and electromagnetic environment as well as they desired. During this time they incorporated small amounts of genetic material from the primates to assist them in assimilating to Earth's environment. Over generations their DNA changed slightly, allowing them to become more adapted to Earth.

While these Earth-Lyrans were incorporating primate genetics into themselves, other groups of Lyrans were on the planet to carry out the Founders' wishes as well as their own by inserting Lyran genetics into the primates. The arrival of these Lyrans refueled the conflicts the Earth-Lyrans initially escaped from, so they chose to find another planetary system to colonize. Desiring to build a new culture where they could become isolated from old conflicts rooted in their past, they explored the region widely before they decided on an open cluster of young blue stars known as the Pleiades.[1]

When the Pleiadian star system began to be colonized by Earth-Lyrans it was intended to be a very balanced, independent race. This was reflected in their choice of a new, stable star cluster. More than anything else, they desired to create a culture based on harmony, truth, and unconditional love. Once the colonization plan became known, those of Lyran descent who desired a new home decided to colonize other areas of the Pleiades star cluster as well.[2]

These early Pleiadians (the previous Earth-Lyrans) possessed highly developed intuitive skills, as well as an inbred desire to create a community lifestyle. The Whole was as important as the Self. Even with this desire, it took these beings generations to mature and create their own identity separate from their Lyran roots. For generations they developed this new culture which was philosophical in nature and technologically progressing at a rate perfect for their development. Though there were several periods of conflict, the cultural base that these new Pleiadians created remained stable for many thousands of years.

---

1 Splinter groups also colonized other systems in Earth's galactic neighborhood.
2 Visibly, we only see seven stars in the Pleiadian system. From the Pleiadian point of view, there are hundreds of stars with habitable planets (some unseen from Earth), which make up the Pleiadian colonies.

Over generations the community-oriented Pleiadians began to favor peace and tranquility so much that they learned to invalidate all forms of negativity. Deeper and deeper they submerged their natural humanoid tendencies, until a great emptiness appeared within their being. There was no conflict, resolution, or learning. A voice cried out from within them. There was a portion of them that desired to be heard.

From this well of despair they reached out to their Lyran forefathers. When the call was answered, the Lyrans were surprised to find a culture that had virtually cut itself off from creation. The Pleiadians had no knowledge of what was occurring in the universe around them. They were unaware of the anguish of Orion, even though they were both descendants of Lyra.

When the Pleiadians were made aware of the Orion struggle, their own sleeping dragon awakened. They felt a passion. Once again they felt alive; a deep mission was sparked within their souls. They offered to be of service within the Orion struggle. It was then that they committed themselves to fighting the Orion negativity.

Thus it began. They entered the Orion struggle through many vehicles. Some souls chose to incarnate directly into the system within both polarity orientations (positive and negative) in order to understand the struggle. The majority of these Pleiadians incarnating into the Orion struggle became ensnared—it is easy to enter the Orion reincarnational cycle but virtually impossible to escape. Others chose to ally themselves with the Black League or continue to incarnate within the Pleiadian system and attempt to contain the expansion of the Orion Empire. They fought with every ounce of their being against the negativity they saw around them. Unconsciously they also fought the negativity still further—within themselves.

The struggle continued. The Pleiadians fought as zealously against the Orion negativity as they did their own latent shadow selves. Instead of finding a truth within, they only perpetuated their hatred of their own negativity. It was only when the Orion Empire destroyed one of their populated planets that they disengaged themselves actively from the Orion struggle. The lifeless, charred planet still stands in their system as a reminder of their past actions. When that planet was obliterated, the Pleiadians were devastated. Finally, an impasse was reached.

On the highest levels of being, every consciousness involved in the Orion drama took a step back. They evaluated the situation. It became obvious that the resolution needed to occur from a different angle. They agreed to extend the conflict to another arena within the galaxy. The Pleiadians were faced with a choice: would they return their energies to their home worlds, or would they agree to resolve their own issues (as well as the Orion struggle) once and for all?

Initially, they chose to return home. This allowed them to gather their strength and search the very depths of their souls to find a way to become whole. They were so afraid of the negativity that they became immobilized. They waited. They pondered ... and they faltered.

While they waited, the Inception project began in full force upon the Earth. The Lyrans were the physical directors of the project (under the Founders), accepting assistance from other physical groups such as the Sirians. It quickly became apparent that they needed a genetic structure of terrestrial as well as extraterrestrial origin for their Inception project. They contacted the Pleiadians.

At first the Pleiadians expressed reluctance about becoming involved with Earth once again. However, the Lyrans pointed out possible Pleiadian benefits with a deft craftiness. Knowing that the Pleiadians had originally incorporated Earth primate genetics into themselves, the Lyrans admitted that they needed certain aspects of Pleiadian DNA for the developing terran species on Earth. Unknowingly, they also created a way for the Pleiadians to face their negativity once and for all.

It was proposed that a DNA transfer from the Pleiadians into the terran species over a long period of time would create a race of humanoids who would be terrestrial but would also have extraterrestrial roots. The closest ancestors of these Earth humans would be the Pleiadians, and through these family ties the Pleiadians would be allowed to be involved with the Earth species development. During this involvement they would observe the developing race, interact intermittently in order to keep them on course, and learn about human negativity. This vicariously would heal the pain of the Pleiadian past. After some reluctance to associate once again with the Lyrans, a group of Pleiadians finally agreed.

From this agreement came thousands of years of Pleiadian interaction with nearly every primitive culture upon the Earth. Drawings of space beings and spacecraft adorn many cave walls, and many ancient documents record the actions of these gods who came from the sky. They saw themselves as "gods" no more than today's humans do. However, from the point of view of a primitive people, they surely must have seemed like gods.

During certain developmental stages of a humanoid species, it is common to give up personal power to a godlike or magical figure. This became widespread, and soon the Pleiadians began to relish the power they were given. They began to wield it. Some began using fear in order to manipulate. Their soul-level agreement to learn from the developing Earth transformed into a satiation of personal desire. Many ancient myths concerning jealous gods are directly linked to these extraterrestrial beings from other systems, including the Pleiades.[3]

When these power binges occurred, it was necessary for these extraterrestrials to be reminded of their purpose. Very often resentment built up on the part of the Pleiadians toward other visiting groups. For a period of a few thousand years the Pleiadians grew in power, and then were consistently reminded of their place. The irony of the situation soon became known to them—they had wished to get in touch with their negativity. Their wish had been granted.

During these interactions the Pleiadians involved with Earth were all from the same time continuum. Their contacts were consistent with their development. They had not yet mastered the complex technology of time/space manipulation. It wasn't until the twentieth century that Earth has begun to pull in Pleiadian contact from many different time frames simultaneously.

Though contact continued intermittently until the present day, it has slowed in comparison to earlier times. Most Pleiadians no longer consider Earth humans to be children, and they allow humanity to make its own choices. Once Earth began its technological era, it was watched very closely for the critical mass necessary to activate the DNA code for preservation of the species. Since the 1940s both physical and nonphysical extraterrestrials have been monitoring humanity and attempting communication, mostly in subtle ways. The Pleiadians were

---

3 Examples of these myths include the Egyptian accounts of Set and Osiris, as well as the Sumerian conflicts between Enlil and Enki. These seem like archetypal battles; many cultures have legends of similar figures that can be considered counterparts or perhaps an interpretation of one original story.

the first to begin a major benevolent contact program physically with Earth. Although this was quietly carried out as early as the 1930s, it began to be noticed on a wider scale in the 1970s.[4]

In the 1970s, a Swiss man named Billy Meier documented hundreds of hours of communication with the Pleiadian cosmonaut Semjase. He also possesses a large number of photographs of the Pleiadians' spacecrafts which, using photographic technology, have never been proven to be false. He claims to have been taken both backward and forward in time by the Pleiadians (and their allies the DALs) to view various events.

This contact has caused major controversy since it was revealed. Meier had been provided with evidence (by the Pleiadians themselves) such as a metal sample which was analyzed on film by a noted IBM scientist. The analysis revealed an unusual combination of materials including a rare and expensive element called thulium. Also, when analyzed further, the sample seemed to display properties of both metal *and* crystal. The metal sample subsequently disappeared, but the film analysis remains.

Within the UFO research community this case is a classic example of throwing the baby out with the bathwater. Because it is "too easy," it is considered to be fraudulent. When Meier attempted to construct models of Pleiadian spacecrafts to see if the photographs could be faked, the models were found, and the whole case was labeled a hoax.

The teachings of the 1970s from Semjase and her associates are now beginning to be more widely known. They teach spiritual truths as well as give a partial history of the Pleiadian race. Some teachings warn of impending natural and man-made disasters connected with a new age to come. It seems that these Pleiadian beings were from an orientation in their history where warning humans about approaching cataclysm was part of their contact philosophy. Though these teachings may have been applicable when they were given, one may question how they relate to today's mass consciousness.

There are indications that the mass consciousness of Earth made a shift from a future of disaster to one of increasing responsibility during

---

4   There are indications that negative groups (such as the Sirians) began contact in the 1930s as well and that their negative actions were always countered by more benevolent groups such as the Pleiadians. This heavy contact activity (by both positively and negatively oriented groups) appears to occur in 20-year cycles: 1930s, 1950s, 1970s, 1990s, and as we may perhaps see, the 2010s.

the time period of 1980–1982. Since these Pleiadian teachings were given before the shift was made, perhaps they represent an old idea. It does not necessarily mean they are not valid, but it does mean that perhaps there is a different outlook coming to humanity instead—one which reflects the choices and changes humanity has recently made on a mass-conscious level.

The Pleiadian contact coming to us presently (both in physical and telepathic forms) may echo a different voice. Some claim to be the future descendants of Meier's Pleiadians. These Pleiadians speak openly of their difficult past and why they felt they needed to use certain tactics in dealing with Earth. They admit to having their own motivations for contact, and thank this planet for all they have learned. They are helping society to shed light on other forms of contact in which they themselves are not directly involved (such as negative abduction experiences). They are sincerely assisting humanity by whatever means they can, allowing the planet to achieve a global as well as galactic viewpoint.

The Pleiadians have specific reasons for being tentative in their present interactions with Earth. For thousands of years they have stepped in either to protect us from danger or to control us like children "for our own good." Some splinter groups even manipulated humankind for its own purposes. This has been a source of great shame to them. They now realize that humanity must make its own choices and they must trust the human ability to do so. They have created a karmic cycle through their interference. For their own growth, it is imperative that this cycle be relinquished. The thought of perpetuating the pattern of interference on Earth is the single most fearful idea facing a Pleiadian.

Will Pleiadian contact with Earth continue in the future? Since they are the most similar to the Earth human physically (in fourth-density form), it seems appropriate that they become one of the first to walk this planet undisguised. They stress, however, that as much as humanity might want to meet its cousins from the sky, they will not initiate an open contact program until humanity can embrace its brothers across the street. It is up to this planet. It is humanity who is calling the shots. Are we finally ready to let go of the fear of recognizing our heritage and accept their outstretched hands?

7

The Gateway of Arcturus

Verily, when a person departs from this world
he goes to the wind.
It opens out there for him like
the hole of a chariot wheel.
Through it he mounts higher.
He goes to the sun.
It opens out there for him like the hole of a drum...
He goes to the moon...
He goes to the world that is without sorrow...
　　　　　　　　　　—Brihad-Aranyaka Upanishad

When passing through the Prism of Lyra, there were some beings who decided to remain in nonphysical form. These beings lovingly chose an existence of service to those of the more dense realities, such as third-density Earth. They realized that on developing physical worlds the evolving life may need assistance from other realms. This assistance would come in the form of archetypes, angels, guides, and unseen inspiration.

These beings were attracted to the area of the star Arcturus. During their initial attraction the star field in the Arcturus region was slightly different from its present manifestation, but the energy of the area remains constant. There is a gateway or crossroads in the fabric of time and space in the general area of Arcturus. These beings soon realized this gateway passed dimensionally through almost every other area inhabited from the Dimensional Infusion. It was then that they began to understand their purpose – to aid consciousness from many levels of awareness.

The Arcturan purpose is multifaceted. One idea is that they serve humanoidkind as an ideal. They represent the future self of an individual or a society. Their energy is, by its nature, a magnet that draws out positive potential and integration from the very depths of being. They reflect to Earth where it is heading in its evolution. Once humanity evolves into nonphysicality, the ideal goal is to achieve a consciousness similar to that of the Arcturan mass consciousness. They recognize themselves as a group matrix, committed to the idea of the evolution of consciousness.

Very often Arcturan beings will manifest to humans as angels. It is known that one of the purposes of an angel is to serve humankind. In a very real sense, the Arcturans have a dedication to humanoidkind. They have chosen to learn about physicality through physical beings.

They are etheric in nature. Their energy can be felt as a presence, a surge of creativity or unconditional love. They will manifest according to the belief system of the person with whom they are interacting. To the more traditionally religious, it will be as angels. To some of the more modern seekers, perhaps as extraterrestrials or future selves. Either way the outcome is the same—an interaction with a truly loving being devoted to the service of physical beings and thus the Whole.

Because they serve physicality they interact not only with the humanoid beings upon a planet, but also with the unseen kingdoms whose evolution is different from that of humanoids. Each planet has its own devic kingdom—the consciousness energy of the plant, mineral, and animal kingdoms—and the Arcturan energy acts as a higher aspect of a planet's devic kingdom. Again, they repeat the idea of reflecting the future evolutionary ideal.

There are a small number of Arcturans who choose to experience physicality in order to serve. Rather than entering physicality through the birth process, they choose to "walk in" an already existing body on a physical world. They do not have the need (or the "karmic compulsion," so to speak) to enter through the incarnation process. By various agreements between souls, a "trade" is established. The soul of a human who is emotionally in pain will enter the Arcturus realm for healing, and the curious Arcturan will temporarily embody upon a planet.[1]

The primary service the Arcturans provide for physical beings is that of emotional healing. Arcturus is more of a realm than an actual place, and within the realm of Arcturus Earth souls who have had traumatic deaths (or lives) are healed and rejuvenated. Because the gateway of Arcturus connects dimensionally with Earth, *all* who incarnate on Earth must pass through the Arcturus realm before they reach the planet, unless they consciously choose not to. This provides a healing for those about to be born, and a strengthening of their choices and desires for the physical life about to occur.

The gateway of Arcturus prepares nonphysical consciousness for the intense focus of physicality and thus sexuality. From the Arcturan point of awareness, physicality and sexuality are the same expression. The Arcturus energy is particularly adept at various forms of sexual healing, such as in the case of sexual abuse during childhood or adulthood. The healing energies of Arcturus are equally nurturing for the abused and the abuser, for both are in much pain. The utilization of the Sirius/Arcturus healing matrix can be quite powerful in such cases.

The cetaceans, especially dolphins, can represent the Sirius/Arcturus matrix to those in pain. Since dolphins are quite sexual and unconditionally loving in their expression, they can serve as a physical manifestation of the Sirius/Arcturus healing matrix. This matrix is totally nonthreatening, providing subtle healing on very deep levels.

At death the human consciousness passes through the Arcturus realm. There they are nurtured and cared for until they awaken to their greater reality. In the case of traumatic death, a great tenderness and healing is shared so that the soul about to awaken makes a smooth transition.

In after-death experiences the light that is perceived at the end of a tunnel is actually a representation of the Arcturus vibration. This vibration will be translated through the perceiver's own belief system. Because Arcturus is primarily sixth density, it is often perceived as the Christ or Buddha vibration. The light can be equated with the future or

---

1 This is not a common experience. Many who claim to be "walk-ins" have experienced a more common process that can be called a "soul braid." This process is the bringing in of a higher frequency of the soul's *own* energy, *not* an exchange of consciousness. It can be mistakenly understood as the entrance of a new consciousness, whereas it is a stepping up and integration of the original consciousness.

higher self (Christ self) of an individual. So in a sense, during the death process one is merging with the higher self, which happens to share a frequency range nearly identical to the Arcturus realm. There healing occurs. In all of creation there is nothing that heals, nurtures, and rejuvenates the human spirit as completely as the Arcturus vibration.[2]

Another idea that is synonymous with the Arcturus vibration is the idea of creativity. When one is creating, one aligns with the energy of the Creator. Since Arcturus serves as a "messenger" of the Creator, so to speak, the vibrations are quite similar. In this way Arcturus has been intimately bound to humanity from the beginning, since humanity is always creating.

Arcturus is much more than a star. It is a frequency that one possesses within. It is a frequency of creation, healing, and evolution. It has been with Earth and other developing physical planets from their inception. It is less a character in the galactic family story than an undercurrent— one that is ever present in the entire Dimensional Infusion idea.

Because the energy of Arcturus is an undercurrent that consistently interacts with us, the Earth planetary environment often translates Arcturan energy into a form that is meant to trigger individuals emotionally. An example of this is the lenticular cloud, a spectacular cloud formation that molds itself into a disk shape. It may look like a spacecraft, but most of the time it is merely the Earth environment translating the energy it perceives at an etheric level. These etheric "ships" serve once again to remind humanity of its unseen connections.

Within polarized reality Arcturus has chosen a counterpart to reflect other aspects of its evolving nature. Its counterpart is the area called Antares. Within the dimensional gateway or crossroads there is a joining between Antares and Arcturus which serves as a major focal point of energy in this region. Most of the consciousnesses who incarnate on Earth pass only through the Arcturus vibration. There are others who choose to pass through Antares before they reach Arcturus. These are the individuals who work directly with mass-consciousness patterns, matrices, and cellular evolution.

---

2   In many after-death experiences individuals have spoken poignantly of the bright light they encounter. An account chronicled in Moody's *Life After Life* states, "A brilliant white light appeared to me. The light was so bright that I could not see through it, but going into its presence was so calming and wonderful. There is no experience on Earth like it." Entering the Arcturus vibration after death can be equated with this experience.

Antares is also the dimensional connection point between Earth s quadrant of the Milky Way and the galaxy Andromeda. The Antares/Andromeda connection energizes the abstract concepts of existence and consciousness necessary for physical races to begin to remember their heritage, thus transmuting their past.

Most of the other races explored in this work have more individualized agreements with planet Earth. The Arcturus connection is very fluid, very malleable, but no less important. If one likens all the other characters of the story to ingredients in a cosmic soup, one can see how they all add to the flavoring. However, if one likens Arcturus to the consistency of the bouillon in the soup, it is apparent how the Arcturan vibration is a vital ingredient that holds it all together.

Many manifestations of the Arcturan energy on Earth can be explored. First, one can say that Arcturus and Sirius form a partnership. Whereas Arcturus works with emotional healing, Sirius facilitates physical healing. The Egyptians knew these connections and called upon the energies of the Arcturus/Sirius matrix for assistance in their rituals. The Egyptian deity known as Anubis was a direct Sirian archetype, but worked with the Arcturan energy. Anubis guided individuals into the underworld (the astral), or through the process of physical death. There the energies of both Sirius and Arcturus began the healing process with the soul. The representation of the jackal (or the "dog," as in the Dog Star of Sirius) as Anubis is a blatant signal that the Egyptians were aware of the connection. Anubis (as a Sirius archetype) led the departed soul to the Arcturus realm where healing occurs.

Arcturus represents integration as much as Orion represents the conflicting or polarized nature of humanity. The archetype of Merlin has often been labeled a bridge. When two polarities attempt a unification, there must be a common ground they both stand on before the merging occurs. Merlin is thus a bridge between the explosive Orion and the healing Arcturus. He is the common ground. It is apparent how his energy has been of major importance, not only to Earth, but to all who experience polarity. Magic is the spark created from the friction between polarities that ignites transformation.

Early in the development of Earth, the Arcturans agreed to densify themselves enough to be perceived temporarily. They interacted with the early culture called Lemuria by teaching healing skills. The memory of these interactions was carried throughout generations. When the Lemurians migrated to many areas of Earth, these memories were carried with them. The statues of Easter Island are one of the few ideas that remain in the physical of their direct interaction. These statues are not meant to represent these densified Arcturans so much as to pay tribute to them. The position of the statues is skyward, gazing at the horizon, waiting for the Arcturans' return.

Humanity has never had to wait for their return. The energy has been present all along. If one looks inward instead of outward, they can be found. They are the human race evolved to its highest potential. They remind humanity and edge it forward into the magnificent spiral of evolution. Home is where the heart is, and the heart is the path of Arcturus.

8

Earth Inception

Then God said, "Let us make man
in our image, in our likeness ... "

—*Genesis 1:26*

I n whose image were Earth humans made? Many of Earth's oldest scriptures imply that human development was guided by gods who descended from the sky. Even anthropologists are aware of the unusually fast development of *Homo sapiens*. Some anthropologists estimate that the species *Homo sapiens* appears to be millions of years ahead of schedule.

Whereas the evolutionary development between Advanced Australopithecus and Neanderthal took more than two million years, evidence has been found on Earth that *Homo sapiens* (Cro-Magnon) emerged approximately 35,000 years ago. What is even more intriguing is that while the remains of man are continually discovered, archaeologists have found remains from an even *earlier Homo sapiens* in the areas of western Asia and Northern Africa. These remains date back 250,000 years *before* Cro-Magnon man. It should be stated here that *Homo sapiens* has no evolutionary precursor. Nothing evolved *into Homo sapiens*—the species simply *appeared*.

Would extraterrestrials be interested in having a hand in Earth's evolution? If so, what could they gain from Earth humans? Perhaps it was a way for them to accelerate their *own* evolution.

It seems evident there were three main groups that orchestrated the Earth Inception. We identify them as: the Founders, a Lyran group, and a Sirian group. The Founders facilitated the Inception from a point of nonphysicality and were the "overseers" of the entire project. Unaware of these nonphysical influences, the Lyrans physically orchestrated the Inception and employed a Sirian group to assist. Each group had its own motivations for their involvement. Though the motivations were different, the goal was the same—the creation of a humanoid race on Earth.

As stated earlier, the Pleiadians involved themselves in Earth's evolution for their own benefit. They felt that if they interacted with humans, not only would they be able to be a part of the development of their previous home, but they could learn about negativity and integration without having to incarnate directly into a world that was playing out those ideas. They were persuaded by the Lyran group, who were well aware of the genetic compatibility of the Pleiadians with the new Earth humans being developed.

The Lyran group (a combination of various Lyran races) was always experimenting. Just as humans have certain instinctive drives (such as procreation), these extraterrestrials carry their own drives which emulate *their* "creators"—the Founders. The Founders' "offspring" instinctively carried on with genetic seeding. These Founders were well aware that inbreeding would cause a race to die out, and thus they continually sought new stock to keep the gene pool mixed.

There was another primary Lyran motivation for their involvement with Earth. After eons of conflict within the Lyran offshoot races (Vega, Sirius, Orion, etc.), they were tired of creating civilizations that were polarized and failed to exist peacefully. They were determined that Earth was to be a planet founded on integration rather than polarity. The Lyran group felt that perhaps what they needed all along was a planet whose *beginnings* were integrated rather than one that was carrying the seeds of polarity from other star systems. With this in mind they began formulating their rigid plan for the Earth Inception.

The Founders, however, had other plans. They knew Earth was possibly going to be the final ground for healing the Orion drama, and therefore *must remain polarized* in order to resolve the conflict. The Founders knew that the galactic family might finally learn about integration through the experience of polarity resolution on Earth. The Founders allowed the Lyran group to carry out their plan because they knew it would eventually support the *cosmic* plan.

As for the Sirian group, their motivations were much closer to home. They considered Earth to be within the Sirius trinary star system; thus they believed they had a right to manipulate Earth genetics. The Sirians were interested simply in establishing primitive humanoid races on Earth that could serve as manual laborers while they expanded their colonies to include Earth. Thus they supported the Lyran project with their own goals in mind. The Earth Inception project began.

For many thousands of years during the early phases of the Earth Inception project, the Lyrans[1] watched the developing primate race on earth with cautious eyes. Occasionally they took samples and made slight alterations to the DNA structures. At critical points in development they began inserting genetic material from the Pleiadians[2] (and other groups) into these primates. Over long periods it became increasingly apparent that evolution was accelerating at a rapid pace. When this became evident, the crucial prototype experiments were initiated.

The story of Adam and Eve is one of the few legacies left that can subtly remind humanity of its beginnings. The tale contains many symbolic references to the saga that occurred concerning the type of species who were to inherit the Earth.

As stated, the Lyran group wanted a species founded on integration. Therefore, they felt that the species must have no knowledge of polarity—or "good" and "evil." They strictly controlled the environment of these new humans so they would stay focused on developing as perfect vehicles of integration. They did not want the new humans to *become like them*—polarized. What the Lyran group did not acknowledge was that they were also restricting choice on the part of these new humans to manifest their own destiny.

---

1   These Lyrans, as well as others, have been known by the Hebrew term "Nefilim," erroneously translated as "giants." Nefilim literally means "those who have come down." Genesis 6:4 states: "The Nefilim were on the earth in those days—and also afterward—when the sons of God went to the daughters of men and had children by them. They were the heroes of old, men of renown." The original Hebrew term translated as "renown" is "shem," which literally means airborne vehicle, possibly rocketship. Hence, "they were the heroes of old, people of the rocketships."

2   As implied previously, the Pleiadians carried Earth genetics that successfully integrated into Lyran stock. Thus they became the ultimate choice to see the terran race on Earth.

After generations of working with primates and extraterrestrial genetics, the Lyran group developed a human prototype whose meaning, "of the earth," has been translated into the name "Adam." The Adam prototype was introduced on Earth to test its environmental adaptability in many areas of the planet. (There were many Adams). When this prototype was satisfactorily adapted, the Adams were recalled.

"So the Lord God caused a deep sleep to fall upon the man, and he slept. Then He took one of his ribs [or part of his side], and closed up the flesh at that place."[3] Through cloning and genetic engineering, a female prototype was created that is translated as "Eve." Both were returned to the environment and watched closely.

Out of their desire to create a species that had no knowledge of polarity, the Lyrans instructed all who tended the prototypes to forbid them knowledge—to actually deny them the right of choice which all divine beings are granted. Hence, one can see the meaning of the statement by God: "From any tree of the garden you may eat freely; but from the tree of the knowledge of good and evil [polarity] you shall not eat, for in the day that you eat from it you shall surely die."[4]

The Sirians working with the Lyran group disagreed with this philosophy. They felt the Lyrans' personal desires for creating this species was misaligned with the rights of humanoid forms. These Sirians, although wanting to develop the human race for their own purposes, discovered they had a genuine affection for the new humans. Despite this duality they decided to intervene, thus inadvertently giving humans the opportunity to choose.

The Sirian group warned the humans: "And the serpent[5] said to the woman, 'You surely shall *not* die! For God knows that in the day you eat from it your eyes will be opened, and you will be like God, knowing good and evil.'"[6] Being presented with choice and the need for a decision involving their existence, the humans achieved third-density

---

3 Genesis 2:21.

4 Genesis 2:16.

5 The serpent is an archetypal symbol that is found in many ancient myths. The serpent's nature consistently portrays duality—it is feared but yet is a strong ally for humankind. In the Sumerian texts, Enki, the god (Sirian) who protects humanity, is also portrayed as a serpent. The judgment that the serpent is "evil" is more contemporary and may have been a ploy used by the gods (Lyrans) to keep humanity in fear and thus from following the instructions of the Sirians who were attempting to assist humankind.

6 Genesis 3:4.

consciousness. When the humans realized they had been deceived by "God" they opted for knowledge. *Once they made the choice to receive knowledge of polarity they were fully anchored in the physical.* They now possessed ego, or knowledge of "I am," and became self-aware.

"Then the Lord God said 'Behold, the man has become *like one of us,* knowing good and evil [polarity]. He must not be allowed to reach out his hand and take also from the tree of life and eat, and live forever.'"[7] Needless to say, the Lyran group was not pleased. In their anger they denied humans knowledge from the tree of life (Divine Heritage). The human race was thus forced to develop without the knowledge of its connection to the galactic family and the Whole. It would truly be a challenge.

To ensure that the humans did not seek this knowledge, the Lyran group employed some precautions: ". . . at the east of the garden He stationed the cherubim, and the flaming sword which turned every direction, to guard the way to the tree of life."[8] They left humanity its heritage—the legacy of Orion (symbolically portrayed as the sword), without leaving any knowledge of its resolution.

There are suggestions in the ancient Sumerian texts that the cherubim are actual mechanical or robotic devices which, in this case, protect the tree of life. What is the literal translation of the tree of life? In Sumerian the word for the tree of life was GISH.TIL. GISH meant a man-made device; TIL meant (and still does today in contemporary Hebrew) missile. Instead of an actual tree, this may mean the "vehicle to life"—or a spaceship. In Sumerian renderings there are clear depictions of rocketships, as well as men saluting these rocketships. It seems clear that the action by the gods of stationing the cherubim to keep humans from the tree of life was actually denying the humans the knowledge of their heritage. No longer would the Earth human be allowed to openly intermingle with the gods or leave the planet with them. Humans were banished from the heavens.

What happened to the Sirian group who interfered with the plans of the Lyrans? By interfering they became energetically tied to the development of Earth. They have always had many tricks up their sleeve, and in this case they got the last laugh. When working with the Lyran group during the genetic program, they inserted a latent DNA

7   Genesis 3:22.
8   Genesis 3:24.

code within the human cells. This code is triggered by an accelerating vibration that occurs when a civilization begins to evolve spiritually. As Earth accelerates toward self-awareness and fourth density (which is occurring presently), the code is activated. Once activated, the human race unwinds its limited vision like a coil until the expanse of All That Is becomes visible. It was their way of allowing humanity to eat from the tree of life after all.

From these early seeders of planet Earth, humanity has been left a challenge. As stated, the "children" who are seeded usually carry the genetic codes and deep-seated attitudes of the "parents." If indeed Earth was seeded from a point of inequality and lack of free will, might this not explain why humans of many races today still carry an underlying belief in the superiority of the Caucasian/Aryan race (the Lyran group)? Could it be that the very roots of racial bigotry go as far back as the seeding of the planet? The earliest texts available to the seeker certainly suggest this. The Sumerian records give reference to the "black-headed ones" who worked the mines of Africa for the gods. If this is the case —that humanity carries the patterns of its forefathers—then this challenge is just beginning. Breaking free from this godspell that has been cast over humanity may be the key to the liberation of the human race on Earth.

In Earth's past the human race has received conflicting signals from the gods. There were times (some of which are recorded in the Sumerian texts, such as the great flood) when humans were abandoned and left to die on the planet while the gods they trusted left in their spaceships. During these times some gods "illegally" rescued chosen humans. This has created an emotional encoding within the human species during times of crisis. The encoding remembers both of these patterns and a struggle is activated between the fear of abandonment and the joy of salvation. It is imperative that the human race resolve this dependence on the gods and become self-sufficient.

On present-day Earth, extraterrestrial groups whose encodings are rooted in the past still promise salvation. They come to humans as physical space beings or speak telepathically to those who can hear their frequency. Often they name various Earth humans "commanders" or "chosen ones," and continue to tempt the human ego to perpetuate its *own* feelings of superiority. Though these off-planet groups mean well for the most part, they continually perpetuate the gap between the fear of abandonment and the joy of salvation, thus encouraging the separative belief in elitism. As humans take their own power and enter planetary adulthood, those remnant groups will transform as well. The majority of other extraterrestrial groups have learned from their past actions and desire a resolution of this conflict once and for all.

From the point of view of the Founders, the Plan was continuing perfectly. The Lyran group needed to play out the scenario for their own growth. These early extraterrestrial "gods" left behind clues on Earth that will eventually assist in awakening the planet to its heritage. As humanity awakens to this knowledge, it will begin to bring into play the tools that are needed to resolve the Orion drama. Resolution comes from allowance. If the human race can truly allow diversity within unity from a point of nonjudgment, Heaven on Earth *will* be created.

9

Zeta Reticuli:
Transformation and Awakening

They seek the very depths of the soul.
They seek communion.

—Whitley Strieber

The beginnings of the Zeta Reticuli civilization can be traced back in time to the inception of the Apex planet in the Lyran system by the Founders. Theirs is a unique and poignant development that has significant relevance to the evolution of planet Earth.

The Apex planet allowed polarity, expressed through extreme individualization, to tear them apart. Their technological evolution occurred rapidly, surpassing their spiritual development which prevented them from coexisting peacefully on their world. This imbalance in energy caused the virtual destruction of the Apex planet. From the view of an observer in space, the Apex world was obliterated. From the point of view of the Apex inhabitants, a different story occurred.

The Apex planet became extremely toxic. Pollution and high-level radiation made the planet's surface uninhabitable. The Apexians who survived the catastrophe secluded themselves underground.[1] It was imperative that integration

---

1 This underground seclusion produced various factions of Apexians. The one explored in

occur within this new underground society, lest the cycle of destruction recreate itself. Recognizing its importance, they decided to force integration (fusion) through a total restructuring of their reality.

As the Apex planet approached its destruction, mentality and intellect were so highly developed that it was becoming noticeable in the physical forms of the Apexians. The craniums had increased in size significantly over very few generations. Natural childbirth became less and less successful because the craniums were not passing easily through the birth canal. The females simply could not adapt to the rapidity of cranial growth. Anticipating what may be a species crisis, genetic engineers began learning cloning techniques which could eventually replace the birth process. For the Apexians, this move saved their species – for after the planet's surface became uninhabitable, the Apexians found themselves sterile.

Once they realized they were sterile, the Apexians decided to use it to their advantage. They no longer wanted the type of civilization they once had; they wanted to begin anew. Thus they steadfastly decided to rigidly control the genetics of their future society. Genetic engineers began work on the development of their new race. This race (they believed) would be an integrated aspect of their past.

The first priority was to genetically alter the brain structures to affect emotional expression. They shunned their past expression of passion and chaos; they now wanted order. Their brains were thus altered to output a consistent chemical response to external stimuli. They achieved detachment from their ego structure. Over generations of neurochemical manipulations, the Apexians became a group mind. The individualistic expressions they were once extremely proud of were now gone.

The combination of planetary radiation and the effects of their cloning began to produce a race with little physical variance from one person to the other. In order to utilize the planet's underground environment more efficiently, their bodies were created smaller in stature. In adaptation to the absence of ultraviolet light and natural

---

the present chapter is a more benign race. Others who were more negatively-oriented (and assisted in creating the chaos on the Apex planet) eventually left Apex after thousands of years and settled in areas of Sirius and Orion, most notably Betelgeuse. The negative beings who have present interaction with Earth have been labeled as the negative Sirians and the Grays; they have their own motivations for their interactions with Earth.

sunlight, their eyes began to respond to different frequencies of the visual spectrum. Their pupils mutated to cover the entire eye, and the eyes enlarged to allow more surface space for gathering light.

In response to the lack of fresh food, their bodies eventually adapted to the absorption of certain frequencies of light as nourishment. Their skin became photothermic and photovoltaic, sensitive to light sources in the underground caverns. Salvaged plants and luminiferous underground minerals aided in their nourishment. Many of their organs, such as those of the digestive and reproductive systems, thus began to atrophy. The transformation they underwent touched every aspect of their beings. A new civilization began to emerge.

The force and vibration of the Apexians' previous atomic blasts eventually folded the space surrounding the Apex planet and they emerged "on the other side" of a dimensional doorway. During the underground seclusion which lasted thousands of years, the Apexians had no idea that their planet had changed its position in time and space. It wasn't until they emerged onto the planet's surface generations later that they found the star field had shifted dramatically. It was then that they knew the extent of their actions. The Apex planet had shifted its position (relative to time and space) in the cosmos. It now existed "slightly off" in dimension compared to the worlds they were familiar with. To understand what had occurred and use the knowledge to their benefit, they began to master the science of folding time and space.

The day they finally emerged onto the planet's surface once again, they had become a new species. Like a phoenix rising from the ashes, they had managed to produce transformation from destruction. They were no longer Apexians. They now assumed a new identity, that of One People Reflecting the Whole.

From Earth's point of view, these One People can now be called the Zeta Reticuli.[2] Their planet, through its shift in dimension,

---

2   As stated in footnote 1, there were many factions of Apexians who went underground. While underground, several factions developed themselves into *benign* Zeta Reticuli races. These benign entities are the ones addressed here in chapter 9. The faction discussed in footnote 1 can be considered the negative Zeta Reticuli, who after a shift closer to the Reticulum star system, left the original Apex planet and colonized another planet in the Zeta Reticuli system. They are nearly identical in appearance and can be differentiated only by their vibration or behavior, which is inherently negative or self-serving in nature. Perhaps when contradictory versions of the Zeta Reticuli are seen, humans are actually interacting with the Reticuli from different evolutionary points in their historical timeline,

inserted itself into the vicinity of Zeta Reticuli 1 and Zeta Reticuli 2[3] in the Reticulum Rhomboidalis star group.[4] From that base they began reestablishing their connections with the Founders of Life. To this day they continue to carry out the wishes of the Founders for galactic evolution. What they are just beginning to realize is that they are carrying out their own evolution as well.

Today, the Zeta Reticuli require a way to strengthen their genetic line in order to create a future for their race. After generations of cloning using the same genetic material, they became severely inbred and stagnant in their evolutionary growth. Their race is dying, but their oversoul wishes to continue incarnating in physicality. They are deliberately keeping themselves from transitioning to fifth density in order to leave behind a seed of themselves that can genetically continue to reproduce. This will aid the galactic whole in its evolution.

Recognizing their predicament, they called out to the Founders.

The Founders introduced the Reticuli to a diverse planet that genetically possessed a gene pool from many human-type species as far back as the inception of the Lyran races. Instead of the Reticuli going from civilization to civilization gathering genetic material, they could now get it in one place. This planet is Earth.

The Reticuli were primarily attracted to Earth in the 1940s, when the planet began to possess the technology to self-destruct. They are quite aware that their past represents a future possibility for Earth. Because of their ability to travel through time, they could have gathered genetic material from any time in Earth's past. However, they needed

---

even though they all come from Earth's future. The more negative manifestations might be their past, whereas some of the more harmless interactions might occur from a further evolved state. When they come to humans in the present, it is assumed that they originate from a single point in time. If they are indeed coming to Earth from various points in their development, it would explain the wide range of reported abduction experiences conducted by the same beings.

3   *Webster's Dictionary* defines "reticular" as "like a network; complicated." Some may surely attest that the psyche of the Zeta Reticuli beings is complicated indeed!

4   One of the most famous early cases of UFO abduction that supports the origin of these beings is the Betty and Barney Hill case from New Hampshire. In 1961, Betty Hill was shown a map of a star group during her abduction. Years later she drew this map while under hypnosis. At the time, there was no reference to this group on known star charts. It has since been discovered that Betty's drawing matches a newly discovered star group seen from Earth's Southern Hemisphere. The star group, Reticulum Rhomboidalis (the Rhomboid Net), houses the star group now labeled Zeta Reticuli 1 and 2.

genetic material from a period of Earth's history when civilization stands on the brink of destruction and transformation. This will aid them in their own integrative process. In a sense, it is their way of changing their past. By interacting with present-day Earth, they heal their past and change their future.

Today on Earth they carry out this genetic program. Since this planet has not yet understood or embraced the idea of soul choice, most of the individuals who are participants in this genetic program consider themselves victims. There are thousands of stories of terrorized abductees who are plagued by reoccurring experiences of extraterrestrials who snatch them from their warm beds.[5] Experiences of terror occur because humanity is not yet willing to face its own shadow, which is reflected in the mirror that the Reticuli represent.

The Reticuli primarily seek specific human characteristics that they bred *out* of their race eons ago. One such characteristic is a variability of reaction to external stimuli. To relearn this, they must sample and study human neurochemical reactions to a myriad of stimuli.

Their most common method of studying these neurochemical secretions is by the implantation of an organic probe. These probes are inserted into the head of the abductee through either the nose, eye, or ear cavity. These probes absorb and catalog neurochemical data and are removed periodically for study and then reinserted. Should an individual die, the organic probe can be naturally absorbed by the body.

Not only are they seeking biological information from humans, but they are also seeking emotional learning as well. It has been eons since they parented children. The human nurturing ability is a fascination to them. As they begin altering their neurochemical structures, they will once again be able to respond maternally to their progeny. This is one of the primary reasons why women are abducted and asked to hold hybrid children. These human females are helping to reawaken the maternal and procreational instincts of the Zeta Reticuli.

---

5   Although most abductions are carried out by the Zeta Reticuli, there are isolated incidents of other groups using the abduction scenario for their own purposes. For example, the negatively oriented Sirians, Orions, and those termed the "Grays" very often use terrorizing methods. It is essential that humans learn to differentiate the benign Zeta Reticuli contact from the more malevolent interactions. The authors have explored this topic (and its ramifications for personal and planetary evolution) in much more detail in their book *Visitors from Within.*

Humanity is not only helping *them*—*they* are playing a vital role for Earth as well. The Founders are well aware that Earth's humanity *must* integrate itself on several levels or the scenario of conflict will continue. The Reticuli reflect to the human race one of the most fundamental ideas that it has denied—unity. Humans reflect to the Reticuli their own individuality, which terrifies them. If the gap created by humanity's fears can be bridged, transformation will occur in a most profound way.

The Reticuli are presently acquiring genetic material from *volunteers* who have, on a soul level beyond the ego, agreed to be a part of the awakening of the Earth and the birth of a new civilization. At this stage of the game, fear is still needed on the part of the abductees. On Earth, fear is a primary obstacle to growth. If humanity can move through fear, it will achieve many goals that presently seem out of reach. It will be done through awareness, *not* through the validation of victimhood. The Reticuli need to confront their fear as well (which they still deny), and move through it. Without that fear, growth would be minimal. Sometimes the greatest barriers produce the greatest rewards.

One of these rewards is the creation of a new hybrid race who possess the integrated qualities of the Zeta Reticuli and the Earth human. They will be unified and diverse. They will be rich with humor and fluid with their emotions. Most of all, they will be the unconditionally loving heralds who lead us back to the Source of All.

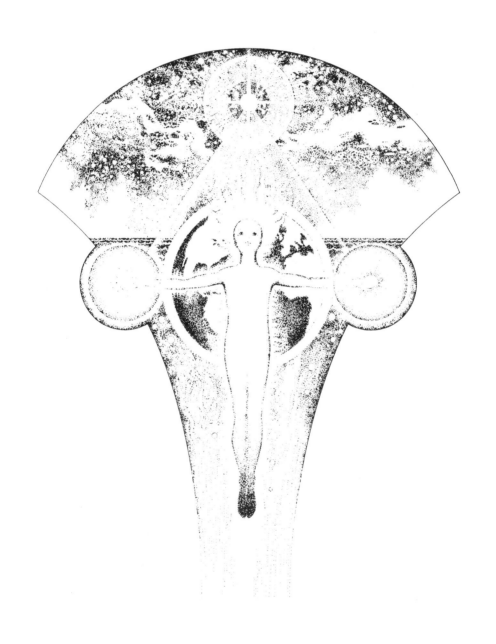

10

Integration:
Coming Home to Ourselves

And while all other creatures from their birth
with downcast eyes gaze on their kindred earth;
He bids man walk erect, and scan the heaven
from whence his soul has sprung,
to which his hopes are given."

—*Ovid*

Integration means the allowance of all levels of being as valid portions of the whole. It means letting go of denial. It means embracing ourselves as well as each other.

Just as our unified consciousness *created* this realm of polarity, we can transform it. When integration occurs, this realm will become defined by very different parameters. We will become the archetypes as well as the Founders. We will shift perspective and become conscious of ourselves as the Creator. It does not necessarily mean that our identities will be absorbed. It could mean that we will awaken to the point where we will consciously choose our destinies, although not from a place of ego. Perhaps we may choose to enter other realms and be the unseen friends for planetary societies still playing the game of separation. We may even be another planet's extraterrestrials—pondering the same decisions regarding interference that our forefathers faced.

In stilling ourselves and listening closely, we can hear and feel the undercurrents of this transformation. Existence and change are the only constants. We can play the game of illusion that we are an accidental creation, but sooner or later we tap ourselves on the shoulder and the game is up. In Earth's reality we have created the Arcturans, Sirians, Lyrans, Orions, Reticuli, Pleiadians, etc., to be the selves who tap us on the shoulder. They are really part of the same one thing—*us*.

So how on Earth do we encourage integration to take place? First of all, *we must know that it will take place with or without our conscious action. The main difference is that conscious action will invite our process of divine awakening to bloom.*

The conscious action that will accelerate our integration process is very simple—allowance. If we *allow* on all levels in which the integration takes place, we will see our paths unfold before us joyously.

Integration will take place on four main levels: Mental, Emotional, Spiritual, and Physical.

MENTAL

For us to integrate our mentality means that we allow ourselves to combine not only our cerebral processes, but our intuitive and emotional ones as well. The kind of thought today that is validated most is almost entirely head-centered. Formulas and calculations determine the reality of twenty-first century Earth. If we can allow ourselves to understand that the intuitive and emotional processes are just as valid and can be used in combination with the mental, we will be well on our way toward integrating our mentality.

EMOTIONAL

Integrating emotionally means that we begin learning how to embrace our shadow self. We can start opening inner closets and digging deep into the subconscious for beliefs which hold us back. More often than not, these neglected parts of ourselves only want attention. As the Pleiadians and the Lyrans before them discovered, denial and separation only prolongs the pain of existence. Let us learn from these other selves on distant worlds. Let us not repeat the same lessons over and over again.

SPIRITUAL

To integrate spiritually is perhaps the easiest of all. Each person possesses an inner spirituality that is not connected to doctrine. If we can release the doctrine and touch the innate spirituality, we begin the integration process. It extends outward onto the planet by the honoring of *every person's truth* as a manifestation of the One Truth. This allows each of us to coexist within our philosophies without needing to change each other's beliefs. The fact that God/All That Is exists is not changed by our argument over which color robe "He" wears, or what his true name is. We are so afraid of being alone and separate that we create even more separation through our need to have a unified doctrine. If we have the courage to begin touching this inner spirituality, we will see our transformation blossom. Our divine nature is already an integrated experience—but can we learn to transcend the mind's ego games and see our true Selves?

PHYSICAL

Integration physically is slightly different. It involves an acknowledgment of our past and our history as being part of a grander scenario on a cosmic scale. From the Source and the Founders we fragmented. We have stretched our individualization to its outer limits. Coming together will require us to once again acknowledge and accept ourselves as part of our galactic family. As we move through our racial fears and stop allowing skin color and cultural differences to be barriers between us, we also move through our fears by celebrating the communion that the Zeta Reticuli offer us. We can allow integration on all levels into our physical life here on Earth.

Not one of us is "from" another place. We are from the Source, and the Source is vast. To say we are "from" the Pleiades is a denial of all the other ideas that we are. Our terrestrial selves become confused if we continually deny that our existence is part of the planet's body. We are of All That Is! If we feel a connection to an off-planet race, we are identifying with what they represent or with various lives we have lived in that system. If individuals insist on stating they are "from" somewhere, the suggestion is offered that they proclaim their alliance with Earth. They have chosen a life *here*. In a very real sense,

Earth people can be seen as models for integration. We are divine and terrestrial; of gods and men. We are proof positive that human life can adapt to seemingly insurmountable circumstances. Let us celebrate *humanity!*

There are no space brothers who are *really* going to save us—they are too busy saving themselves! We are not children. Though we are still playing the game of unawareness somewhat, we are looked at by other civilizations as an enigma. We are the civilization that refused to die! Our resilience and faith in our abilities has continually proven our worth. We refused to be dominated and used by the Lyran group in the Garden of Eden. Various "plagues" by the gods have not succeeded in wiping us out. Thanks to Noah and the Sirian overlord who warned him, we have a flourishing civilization today.

Many have wondered why Earth has been observed by so many extraterrestrial groups. Perhaps we are a predictable demonstration of integration in action. It may be painful, but in our mass conscious belief, pain can produce miraculous results.

Earth of the present and Earth of the future is indeed that miracle. Let us celebrate that miracle by integrating ourselves and taking responsibility for our planetary reality. We are part of an Association of Worlds and our membership is up for renewal! This time, membership requires our awakening to the cosmic drama of which we've agreed to be a part. Our awakening will lead us home ... to ourselves.

Part 2

11

A Galactic Creation Story

The following is an excerpt from a channeling session by Lyssa Royal that explores many themes from the first edition of The Prism of Lyra, *as well as new information that enhances the original material. Audience questions are included.*

Greetings everyone; this is Germane. How are you this day? Excellent. Well, hopefully we will have some fun with you today, and we will attempt to make it not just a bunch of boring information but a lively story to engage your imagination.

Sasha [Lyssa's Pleiadian contact] has talked about polarity and this reality paradigm that you are all a part of and what came "before" this reality paradigm. Who were you? What type of reality were you experiencing? Well, just like Sasha, even though we may have more of a bird's-eye perspective, we are still on this side with you, so to speak, so we do not have much to say about that. What we *do* want to talk about is your state of being as a unified whole before this reality here was seeded or created. This would be more of a state of being in-between reality paradigms. So wherever all of us together were before this paradigm, we passed through that and there was a limbo, if you will. In that limbo, you experienced that reunification from the old paradigm. And in that beautiful, wonderful limbo, you experienced the joy of unification, the bliss, and total oneness—one mind. You would not even be able to separate into individual beings. As humans think of this idea, they might think of it as God. So, in essence, you were in your most integrated God-Self at that point. Please note that we speak of "before" and "after" because linear time is a tool that can be used to explain ideas. However, in truth, everything exists simultaneously.

So you are hanging around in this wonderful blissful God-Self— this integration state—pondering the universe. You are pondering yourself as a great being and thinking, "I wonder what it would be like to not know my Self? I wonder what it would be like to wonder about aspects of 'me.' I wonder what it would be like to not know this bliss of unification."

Any time there is that type of wondering or questioning, thought creates reality. So the force of this question created what you might call an "explosion" or a "fragmentation."

This fragmentation could be likened to a mirrored ball—which was your original state of oneness—suddenly fracturing and becoming like one of those disco balls. You are still basically spherical, but you are kind of cracked and skewed in different directions with each little piece of mirror facing a slightly different way. Because each piece is facing a different way, you don't necessarily have the perspective of a "Whole." At the same time, you don't even realize that the piece of mirror next to you sees reality a bit differently because it is skewed in a different direction. So ultimately what you've done is go from a smooth mirrored ball to the cracked disco ball, so to speak.

We are going to talk about this fragmentation in varying stages so that you can begin to understand a progression of evolution. We are not talking about hierarchy, a concept that only makes sense in a linear reality. The idea of there being humans, spirit guides, ascended masters, and all of that in a hierarchical fashion is or can be important for you to understand various steps of evolution in a linear reality. However, in the scheme of things, there is no hierarchy. There is only what you might call a rainbow—varying frequencies of which none are better or higher. So even though it may seem as if we are presenting some of this information in a hierarchical sense, we do not mean it that way. Furthermore, we are going to ask you to engage your imagination and try to remember throughout this session that we are limited by your physical dimension and may be presenting this in what may seem to be a time stream (past, present, future, or before, now, after), but it is meant to be understood as all existing simultaneously. If your brain twists at the thought of that, just put that concept in your back pocket and pick it up every once in a while. You don't have to intellectually understand it. Just pretend you understand it and that will help.

The First Fragmentation

This great being says, "I wonder what it would be like to not know myself." That force of wondering actually embodies the idea of polarity and shows you how polarity begins. When you wonder about a state opposite to your experience, as this great being did, you create a reality in which there are two states—knowing oneself and not knowing oneself. That is polarity. Explosion. Fragmentation. The mirrored ball cracks.

At first, the mirrored ball cracked in large pieces as a metaphor. The little disco-ball pieces weren't created yet. That one unified God-Self cracked into several group consciousnesses, who begin to become the architects of the reality that they are about to create. We call these initial architects (the initial large pieces of the metaphorical mirror) the Founders. In a sense, they eventually founded physical reality.

Further fragmentation ensued as these group beings began to wonder even more about this reality that they were beginning to learn about—thus more cracks appeared. There were several fragmentations, and yet these beings could still be called Founders. The earliest fragmentations were in the nonphysical realm. As the fragmentations occurred more and more, these beings began to take the appearance of densified light (plasma). There are a number of images that one could use to talk about these Founders. Some have been equated with what people call the "praying mantis beings." Some have been depicted as tall and willowy—looking like a Zeta Reticuli or Gray but meant to be a Founder. These are the first beings densified enough to take physical form, and they begin to act as the architects of the reality that is yet to come.

Obviously we are attempting to relay a story in words that has so many other dimensions to it. We can only do this by using metaphor and imagery in order for you to understand the basic idea. To really know it deep in your soul, use this imagery and metaphor to take you on a journey inside. The feelings and sensations you get inside yourself will actually give you more complete answers than what we can communicate through the limitation of words.

This disco ball still maintains the great love, that great bliss of oneness. The illusion is that it is cracked and can't see parts of itself. Thus it forgets about the intensity of that love. But sometimes there are moments of bliss that remind you of what the unification was.

The Founders

So imagine that you have these Founders—the very first densified beings—who embody this huge amount of love. Without passing judgment, these Founders embody more love than humans can embody at this time. If you were to meet one of these beings, it would be nearly impossible because of the frequency difference. All of you have had communication with these beings because they recognize that you are all part of the same disco ball! These are aspects of your Self on its more integrated levels. Imagine meeting one of these beings. It would force you to rapidly entrain with the frequency of that being. You could not hold this 3D beta-brain-wave-dominated reality. You would thus have to meet in another state of consciousness, such as theta or delta. (We are referring to the brain states: delta being the sleep state and theta being a very deep state that occurs before sleep or in deep meditation. Those brainwaves dictate the reality you experience.)

Many of you have had dreams of these tall, willowy beings—sometimes blue, sometimes appearing as a mantis. Some of you have had what you've labeled as negative dreams or negative encounters with beings that appear to be mantis beings. These are not the ones that we are referring to. We are instead referring to beings on a very high plane of existence. The mantis beings' physical appearance is really only the way humans perceive them. It is not the way they perceive themselves. Keep that in mind.

These beings were responsible for building and seeding the reality to come. It has already been set in motion that this reality will be based on polarity. "I wonder what it would be like to not know myself"—this thought sets the tone for polarity. This is why when the Founders' light densified into a physical form, it assumed a symmetrical form—

two arms, two legs, two eyes, and so on. It is based on symmetry and polarity (male/female). This is not to say that there aren't other life forms that have other matrices. In this current presentation, we are only talking about the life forms that share your galactic lineage.

Stars and Planets

These Founders initially began guiding the creation of stars, solar systems, and so forth. Stars are actually Founders who did not densify in a symmetrical body. Stars are conscious beings who have simply taken a different form. The manifestation of these star beings is representative of the whole disco ball—a reminder to all of you of where you come from. So when you look in the sky at the stars and are so moved emotionally, you are looking at your forefathers. These great beings chose to stay as far away from the manifestation of polarity as possible and to shine light in the void to keep the candle burning within *you* so that you would remember where you come from. Perhaps you will never look at the stars in the same way again!

This brings us to the idea of how some people who are looking at the heavens and see the planet Venus or the star Sirius think they are seeing a UFO. Often these people are sensing the consciousness behind the star or planet, because all of them are conscious. But sometimes the human mind puts a UFO label on the star because it is not really taught that stars are conscious. If you hear people saying that Venus is a UFO, do not judge them too harshly; they are certainly tapping into a consciousness. This idea of the Founders appearing as the stars is the oldest manifestation that you have to remind yourself of where you come from.

It has often been theorized that passing through black holes or the sun can help you access other dimensions or realities. What you are really doing when you allow yourself that type of transport is going back into the void between reality paradigms. It is kind of like a way station. For now, we will not go into that. The point is simply for you to consider the idea that these stars are those Founders who have chosen not to densify themselves into symmetrical bodies.

Now you can see how the architects (the Founders) and the stars cooperated in the creation of the physical universe. It wasn't that these architects went around terraforming civilizations, but there actually was a cooperation of consciousness so that, in the forming of planets, planets become stars that are fragmented. Thus planets, being fragmented star consciousness, also hold the Founder consciousness and they become planet beings. Your planet being is called Gaia, or Earth. You call her a "she." She is a Founder. She is a conscious, living being. She has not chosen to shine the light in the void like a sun, but she has chosen to sustain life in the void in cooperation with those who choose to shine the light in the void.

Now that we have established the identities of planets and stars, let us go back to the architects that have taken on the bodies of light. As they cooperated with the physical creation of the galaxies, it was time to begin populating. These beings are extremely wise. They knew this wasn't going to be a "walk in the park." They knew it would not be a Garden of Eden with a bunch of people living in wonderful joy and bliss, because that is where they came from and the question was, "I wonder what it would be like not to know myself?" Thus they were not going to create a reality where everything is wonderful. They let the natural energies of polarity—the basis of this reality—begin dictating the life forms that began to populate the worlds and the ideologies of these life forms.

There is an area now that you call Lyra that can be considered a cradle of civilization but not the physical stars that are there now. Those are much too new. The ones we refer to are much older stars that were once there and acted as the womb that sourced nearly all of the life forms that became your galactic family.

As the Founders fragmented further, they began to identify themselves with planets with the cooperation of the star Founders and the planet Founders. Once the planets became stable, the very first life forms were not evolved from bacteria onward, though of course that would certainly be possible—it just takes a lot longer than scientists realize. They literally went through a process of even further densification of their plasmic energy so that they began to manifest in bodies in solid, physical, dimensional reality.

So what did these first bodies look like? They were pretty standard— two arms, two legs, very little hair. They were generally large, much larger than you are on Earth. If we were to put a measurement to it, it could be anywhere from 10 to 60 feet with a maximum slightly larger than that. Skin tone came in various colors, including blue, brown, white, yellow, and red—it depended on the different group that manifested. There were two eyes (much larger eyes than you have), a nose (a lot smaller than yours), a mouth, ears (generally smaller than yours), and not a lot of hair. They had very agile bodies—not necessarily really muscular but lean and with an agility like your Earth masters from the East, who have been practicing intense forms of yoga for fifty years. They were very flexible, on the thin side, and very strong, but they appeared weak.

These beings wanted to give reproduction a try, but found that they really didn't have a clue! At first they manifested as androgynous, thinking that they could self-replicate, but they realized that that was not compatible with a polarized reality. It wasn't challenging enough. They then began to separate outward into what you might call male or female. Of course, once that happened, they had to figure out the process of reproduction. They found that reproduction was very difficult and part of the reason was that their bodies were densified plasma and had just come from another realm of being. They were living on a planet that had gone through millions of years of evolution to obtain stability. They were like a foreign entity trying to live as part of an ecosystem from which they did not naturally evolve. Though you might think that something like this could be achieved in a laboratory, it was really very difficult. What they understood was that in order to really fully incarnate as beings on these planetary bodies, they had to incorporate planetary genetics into their genetic structure.

They actually had to wait even longer in the scheme of things, until life forms of a generally primate nature (some reptilian or avian) began to develop. At that point, they could borrow the genetics and incorporate very small amounts within their own body structures. Here is the irony, paradox, and challenge: In your literature, you call this the "Fall." Once they did this, they began to forget who they were.

When you incorporate the genetics of a planetary body, it is kind of like putting a virus into yourself. It multiplies and takes over all of your cells. So when these beings incorporated the matrices of the planetary genetics, their genes were changed. Their cells changed to the point where they began to forget. They could not contain the great amount of light that they could previously. We remember at this time that some of these planetary species became desperate. They were terrified. Some of the beings chose to return to the unification of the Founders because they could not emotionally deal with that level of separation or sense of abandonment. They could not deal with not knowing themselves, which ironically was the reason they wanted to experience separation in the first place.

Some returned to the nonphysical Founder level. Some simply chose to remain until they forgot the connection with their Founder forefathers, beyond understanding it only on an intellectual level. They didn't know how to bring their connections into practice. It was like falling asleep.

These very first planetary civilizations began to forget who they were and now had to focus on creating their own identities out of nothing. They remembered no history, because they did not have one. If you want to feel what abandonment, loneliness, and isolation is, think of these beings with no memory and no history having to build their own identities in total terror of being alone.

This is at the core of every single one of you. Remember, you *are* these beings. You are part of them. This is *your* past. Most of you have not come to peace with that terror of isolation and you carry it inside yourselves. For most of you, it doesn't affect your lives in a negative way, but it is always there. This is where it comes from—the first initial trauma of being alone.

As a side note, when children are born in your reality, they come from a state of much greater integration. When they come into this reality, they fragment very similarly to the way the Founders fragmented. There is a very strong parallel. The older the children get (from birth to around two years old), the more they go through that intense fear of abandonment and isolation again. Not only do you carry this in your soul, but you re-experience the trauma every lifetime that you live.

There are some civilizations that don't experience this to the depth that you do on Earth. The Pleiadians, for instance, have come to peace with it, as well as other civilizations. You on Earth are still connecting with that isolation.

Left to their own devices, these scattered planets with densified Founders who lost their connection and have "fallen" now have to begin building a culture. Since this was a reality of polarity without any external influence, these different planetary groups began building their own self-identities. In the greater scheme of things, they ended up creating two separate ideological polarities. This is no surprise, but they were none too thrilled to discover that manifestation!

One group chose to be the explorers and the pioneers. They were going to traverse the dimensions and planets. They were going to colonize and spread out, asserting their will on reality so that they could conquer this dimension and get back "home" to unification as quickly as possible. They felt that was the way to do it. They were convinced. They didn't want to waste any more time. They were just going to conquer the universe and then go back home.

Lyrans and Vegans

We are moving very rapidly through time here. The actual process was billions of years and it can't be covered in one day. These beings who decided to conquer space and move outward, spreading their seed, are referred to as Lyrans. Don't hold us too rigidly to this. *Generally*, their bodies ended up manifesting themselves as having lighter skin, lighter hair, and lighter eyes—what you might call Caucasian on Earth. As they began to incorporate the planetary DNA, they began to grow body hair. These were the Lyrans.

Within the star group that you now know as Lyra, there is one star called Vega that is fairly close to Earth. In the general vicinity of Vega were the planets that began forming a species identity that was, in some ways, a polar opposite to the Lyran ideology. These individuals believed that the way back home was by going *in*. They desperately wanted to not lose the connection with God (or the Founders). They could not deal with the idea of the isolation. Thus they began trying to reclaim their esoteric knowledge, or knowledge of what you might call God. They were not so much interested in conquering space. They did eventually evolve to the point where they used space travel, but that wasn't their priority.

We are going to give you a very simple analogy to describe what the Vegans are like. Most of you will understand this and it will give you a familiar framework. In the very beloved Earth mythology that you call *Star Trek*, the Vegans are akin to the Vulcans. They had a very high proficiency of telepathy, spiritual connection, physical strength, and so on. Their physicality tended to be to varying degrees darker-skinned, with darker eyes and darker hair. You might see them as similar to the races on your planet known as Native American, Aboriginal, or Asian.

Now you can see the polarities. Polarities began manifesting in skin color, ideology, and just about everything else. When these cultures met, they clashed. The Lyrans were (though they would never admit this) somewhat jealous of the Vegans, because the Vegans really didn't seem to have lost as much of their memory. At least to some degree, they had a level of peace about them because they could remember—if only in metaphor—their origins. That pretty much made the Lyrans angry. That anger was, of course, anger at the Self for losing the connection. The anger was channeled in another direction—more space travel and colonization.

The Vegans, for a time, tried to ignore the Lyrans but it was kind of like when there is a bully at school who keeps goading you. At some point, you want to make yourself stronger. The Vegans began to feel that if the Lyrans are going to continue to be like this, then they had better start learning how to defend themselves.

At first, their ways of learning to defend themselves were not through technology. That was the last thing they would even think of. It would be through consciousness mastery. They began to learn what you might think of now as martial arts. This included various forms of energy manipulation as defense. The Vegans soon realized that they still had to go out into space and develop conventional technology. But wherever possible, they tried to use themselves as the tool rather than the technology.

It might sound like what we are saying is making the Vegans out to be these good, wonderful, spiritual beings and casting the Lyrans as bad, horrible dictators. No. The Vegans had their own very ruthless side as well. And the Lyrans had their own gentle, loving side. We are only taking this stance so you can actually identify the polarity; that is all. You will soon see the ruthless and compassionate sides of both parties when we talk about how these civilizations branched out. There came a point where life began exploding outward for both the Vegans and the Lyrans through exploring and colonization. At that time, space was like a wilderness—there were no other civilizations.

The very first group who came to your Earth solar system in its infancy was the Vegans. When they first came to this solar system, Earth was very different. It was during the very early part of the dinosaur era. The planet hadn't even stabilized very much at all.

The Vegans were particularly attracted to it because they sensed that natural resources were very rich. Also, they were very drawn to the frequency and saw the potential of the solar system because it had so many planets that could be used very easily. When a group came to a solar system for the first time in those days, they would claim it as their own for their "empire." So during the very early reptilian era on Earth, the Vegan colonists claimed it.

Earth and the Solar System

Are there different Founders responsible for the evolution of life on Earth? And are they not necessarily working in cooperation with the colonizing Founders?

At first it was cooperative. When the early Founders still maintained their connection and understood that planets and stars were Founders too, it was a cooperative effort. But as they began to lose their memory, sometimes it appeared cooperative and sometimes it did not. The level of cooperation was pretty much based on the level of memory. Remember—the unified Founders, the "architects," still embrace the whole reality and thus everything that happens is always according to the "plan," or divine will. When there is no memory, it is hard to remember that and thus it looks like there are differing agendas. This is where conflict arises. Whether these new beings remembered or not, *everything* happened (and still does) according to the will of the architects, the Founders, or "God"—whatever word for that you wish to use. The only difference is that memory—do they/you remember or not? Do you/they remember that there really is only *one* being, manifesting through a multitude of fragments?

Is it true that the first colonists on Earth, the Vegans, came here in physical form?

Yes. But the very first time they came—the dinosaur period, when the planet was very unstable with lots of volcanic activity—they weren't colonizing at that point. They were mostly in orbit and would come down. Actually, they first colonized the planet you know as Mars and the asteroid belt *before* they colonized Earth. As you will see when we continue with the story, when they came to Earth, they also did some genetic tinkering with the reptiles. We'll get to that in a moment.

Were they conscious about the consciousness of Gaia when they came here? Or had they forgotten that?

Being that these are Vegans and not Lyrans (said with all respect), they had more of a connection with the sacred. As an analogy, their knowledge of Gaia would be similar to a Native American's or Aboriginal's relationship to the land. There was always an attempt to live in harmony with it at the *beginning*. But then they also lost their memories.

Are you saying that the reptilian energy was one of the first to come, at the time of the dinosaurs?

Let us clarify that the Vegans themselves were not reptilian. They were mammalian, and they were oxygen-breathers who bore their young. When they came to Earth, the most advanced indigenous life here at the time was reptilian and they chose to use some of the genetics of some of the reptiles within themselves. We are going to go further with that a little bit later.

What happens with shooting stars, neutron stars, and so forth?

Some of them are choosing to return home. A black hole, for instance, will be a Founder that has gathered so much experience for the galactic family that it can collapse in on itself and implode and go back to Source. But that doesn't mean it disappears. When it goes back to Source, it creates a wormhole. It still provides functions, but it too evolves and changes. The birth of new stars, quasars, and so on, is a Founder choosing to be "born"—to be of service in that way. A part of that Founder may eventually even find itself in a humanoid body as it fragments further. You are all part of the Founders in a very real sense. You are also part of the stars. We don't mean that just molecularly; you are all tied together. The stars show the varying stages of physical birth and death for the Founders. "Death" simply means transformation.

Was the original thought—"I wonder what it would be like to not know myself?" —the source of the big bang and the creation of the physical universe as we know it?

Yes. Let's say that was the "philosophical" source of it. Of course, what the philosophical source created was polarity. Thus polarity was the scientific source, if you will.

So there wasn't a physical universe prior to that?

No, not in the paradigm that you were about to explore. There were other physical universes, but none operating from the paradigm of polarity. We know this is a lot to stretch the mind around.

Let us go back to the Vegans who came to the Earth system. Their land bases would have been on the planet Mars and on the planet that can be called Maldek (which is now your asteroid belt). Of course, there is Maldek history and Mars history, which is another issue altogether! However, they would take field trips to Earth to conduct all sorts of geological experiments, DNA experiments, and more.

Reptilian Experiments

At one point while they were doing some of their experiments, the Vegans wished to try their hand at some genetic engineering. The only real genetic material they had that was useful for them at that time would have come from the reptiles. They used it with what they considered to be permission. (We mean that they did it in a sacred way, much like a person might do a ceremony. They honored the source.)

Some of them incorporated reptilian DNA within themselves. Some of them did not. You can already see that a new subspecies is forming, so over time you had mammalian Vegans and reptilian Vegans. This is important to remember because they eventually branch off into other star systems in the future. They also did some work in the creation of a race of primarily reptilian beings. They were not master geneticists so they could not really create a straight reptilian being with the type of brain capacity that they themselves had. Instead they had to splice humanoid DNA and reptilian DNA to create a being that was technically a mammal but who appeared reptilian-like.

Now we have three groups (obviously we are passing through time very rapidly). There was the Vegan humanoid group, the Vegan humanoid-reptilian group (who had just a small bit of reptilian DNA), and the reptilian group. Please be clear that these "reptilians" are not reptiles but mammals who appear very reptilian.

Eventually you have these three groups. We are going to have to take you through time quickly now. Eventually the reptilian group migrated outward. The species achieved its own sovereignty and began to move outward into the universe. They settled primarily in the Orion system and also back in some of the home worlds of Lyra that had been abandoned. They didn't stay around Earth very long.

Once the Lyrans and the Vegans began doing genetic engineering, it was usually with the desire and goal of perfecting themselves. It was still understood at this point—even millions of years after the initial fragmentation—that they were still trying to return to the Source, which was now almost mythological. Throughout time, there were varying theories about how one could get back to Source—what is the best way?

For a period of time, there was a widespread theory that if you genetically engineered the perfect vehicle, you could then incarnate the God-Self and thus move back to Source more quickly. In a way, this became a fad. Part of the reason for this genetic engineering was to begin to create the perfect vehicle through which they could incarnate and get back to Source.

In addition to satisfying their own curiosity, the Vegans were also trying to achieve this goal with the original reptilian DNA they were using. It didn't work. Most genetic engineering, up until much later in history, didn't really succeed in terms of evolving the physical vehicle. Of course, the reason for this was because the point wasn't to evolve the physical vehicles. The point was to evolve the Self that incarnates into the physical vehicles. They needed to evolve the Self through various instances of polarity. So it didn't matter what the vehicle was; they weren't going to get back to Source until they had had their fill of the amusement park of polarity.

The Migration

Now we are at a nexus point. The Vegans moved out into Sirius and Orion. The reptilians moved out into Orion and Lyra. The definitions of the species began to cloud. Sometimes they interbred. Let us put our attention on Earth for a moment.

Toward the very end of the reptilian period, there was a great space battle. Earth and its solar system became spoils of war. The Lyrans won. The colonies of Mars and Maldek and the planet of Earth changed hands and became Lyran property. (This has happened several times.) Keep in mind that Vegans had already done some genetic tinkering on Earth. They tinkered with the dinosaurs. They had been tinkering with lower-level life forms that would later have a chance of evolving into primates. The Vegan signature was already on Earth during that very ancient time. But they were forced to leave.

When the Vegans left, they focused a lot of their attention into the Orion system, which at that time was very huge. They colonized a lot of planets. It was a time period of introspection, because what they had felt when they moved to Orion was, "Well, we went to the Earth system. We tried doing what the Lyrans do—colonizing. It didn't work, so let's go within ourselves now." In the very early days of colonizing the Orion system, they went inward and developed their spiritual faculties much more strongly. They began the path of Vegan mysticism.

Vegan mysticism is ultimately the root of several spiritual lineages on Earth, because the Vegans came back later. Vegan mysticism is at the root of many Earth cultures, such as the Tibetan culture prior to Buddhism and the Vedic culture in the area of India prior to Hinduism. This influence was very ancient, and there are just a few ancient texts remaining from this influential time period.

What you have studied on your world about migration patterns and the theory of the migration from Asia over into the Americas is not totally true. Some of it is, but some people were also deliberately moved around the planet. Therefore what you now know to be Native American in North America and Mexico also has a root in Vegan mysticism. This is also why even today there seems to be such a strong connection between Mayan and Tibetan energy. They come from the same very ancient Source. The martial arts (which are more recent), and the ancient Eastern practices that are older but similar (such as yogic practices) were not based in religion but in spirituality. They have their roots in Vegan mysticism as well.

Orion

Let's journey off Earth for now and go to Orion. The Vegans who ended up colonizing there eventually began creating an identity as Orions. Primarily, these particular Orions were darker-skinned with more Asian or Native features and with darker hair. They went through a long period of introspection and development of their spiritual practices. This eventually created a division in which some of these Orions—now having lost their Vegan identities—fragmented their ideology further. Some of them chose to remain in seclusion and develop their practices. Some of them chose to move outward in the Orion system and use spiritual practices as a way to build a great civilization.

We are passing through time very rapidly. Eventually what happened was that the wonderful spiritual practices that had kept the Vegans connected with their God-Selves began to be used and abused. They were forced on to other people who eventually evolved to become one of the most polarized civilizations that ever existed within the galactic family.

So from these humble beginnings, the Orion culture evolved to a point where it had a government that was extremely psychically adept—not just energetically, but technologically as well. They kept absolute supreme reign over the population. They kept the population totally disempowered at every turn.

To give you an example of the immensity of the drama, the Orions eventually created what they call the Orion net. It was an electromagnetic field around their planetary systems that actually trapped the souls of people when they died, so the soul could not leave the system. The net would force the soul to reincarnate back into the system. The idea of Free Will is rampant everywhere, but when you disempower a society and they do not know they have self-determination, they feel as if they have no choice. This is how the Orions were able to maintain this recycling of souls within the system, driving the system further and further into darkness. This reached the point where Orion could not be contacted by other civilizations outside. They totally isolated themselves. Anytime outsiders tried to save the poor victims of Orion, they were destroyed. So the Orion system is where you have all experienced your darkest moments and your deepest sense of disempowerment.

A little while ago we said that the reptilians colonized Orion. They were somewhat associated with this, but they were not necessarily considered Orions. They were a satellite species. They were allowed to come and go and manipulate in their own way. They were not really part of the Orion net. They were not held within the net.

How does a civilization that seems so hopeless like this begin to once again awaken to its own sovereignty? First of all, you had the Orion Empire, which in your *Star Wars* mythology is akin to Darth Vader's Empire. You had the people who were being oppressed and kept disempowered. And then as time moved on, you had a third faction, which were the freedom fighters. These freedom fighters would be likened to the Jedi in your *Star Wars* mythology.

Remember where the Orion civilization came from—Vegan mysticism. Jedis are very real memories of your heritage. They are almost perfectly remembered in your mythology. They were also portrayed in Frank Herbert's *Dune* mythology as the underground freedom fighters called the Fremen. It was the same idea.

There was a huge lesson here. Orion's freedom fighters referred to themselves as the Black League. (Black meant "hidden.") Though the Black League had the purest of intentions—to free the people and bring sovereignty to all, to teach everyone the connection to Source— they felt that the way to fight fire was to use fire. So in their battles with the Empire, they would simply use the same techniques used by the Empire, which of course only generated a bigger fire. It was truly a no-win situation. You cannot ever fight fire with fire and expect that you will get peace as a result.

We are going to give you imagery that may trigger some of your memories. Some of the planets in the Orion system were very desert- like. They had a series of caves and underground tunnels that were mostly formed by lava. Some of them were built. The Black League lived, bred, and had a society in these series of caves. In the *Dune* mythology, this is expressed through the Fremen society, which is a direct Black League memory. Your memories come out in your fiction, so keep your eyes open!

The Empire never really had an idea of how many Black League members there were. They didn't realize for a long period of time that it was a whole society and the population was huge. They were doing all sorts of spiritual practices to disengage the Orion net. In fact, every once in a while they would get some of their priests together to perform rituals and ceremonies to open a hole large enough in the net for one priest's soul to escape and find sanctuary on another world. Sometimes they were successful. The place of sanctuary that they aimed for is what you know as Earth. To them, it was the mythological land of freedom.

In leaving Orion and seeking sanctuary, the priests found Earth. The Empire, realizing that people were escaping, followed them. So Earth is a continuation of the Orion drama, correlating to much of your post-flood history up to present day. It is a continuation in which the people are still seeking sovereignty. Some of the old Empire is still attempting to control people. But as bad as you think it is on Earth, it is *nothing* compared to what some of you endured in the Orion system.

Picture in your mind for a moment living in caves: It is very dry; robes were usually worn, like you see in Earth's Middle East; ceremonies, ritual; and lots of gatherings with deep passion for freedom. In World War II, the Nazi resistance was a parallel. Many of these resistance fighters were ex-Black Leaguers who already knew how to resist an Empire—not just on the surface, but spiritually and energetically.

This is a dark time that many people do not like to go into. This is one of the essential parts of your history. It tells you who you are now, and why you came to be who you are. It helps you remember what the way out really is. The way out will never be fighting. It lies in the integration of polarity.

The Orion Christ

So how did the Orions transcend this tremendous challenge? They were so stuck in the idea of fighting that although they had so many gifts available to them, they could not break the paradigm. Through all of this, please remember that there is an intelligent force—the nonphysical Founders—running the whole show. They were guiding and reminding those who could hear about who they are and what their connections are. During this great dark time in the Orion system, the Founders on the nonphysical level basically said, "We need to send in the paramedics!" It was decided that a Founder would fragment, incarnate in the Orion system, and attempt to turn the whole thing around.

The priests in the Black League knew he was coming through their own methods of prophecy. They also knew that they had to protect the mother of this child. (Does this sound familiar? There are no new dramas under the sun. There is a new stage set, but the story is the same.) The mother was inseminated and put in a very deep cavern on the planet. This cavern was electromagnetically shielded so that she could not be found by the Empire or interfered with in any way. She lived there throughout her entire pregnancy. When the child was born, he had blue eyes. In their culture, only the highest of priests and masters have blue eyes. For them this was a symbol of great mastery.

The child was raised in this environment by the most adept of priests and mystics. But of course the child ended up being the teacher for these priests and mystics! He is known as the Orion Christ.

He served as a teacher for the population of the Black League and he was able —not only through verbal teachings, but through energetics—to help the Black League change this paradigm from one of disempowerment to one of personal sovereignty. If you have a massive population learning to become sovereign both energetically and emotionally, it changes the very fabric of the reality you are in. Thus the Empire began to become less empowered. As the Empire lost its power, the general population (that is, those who were not part of the Black League) began to awaken.

What did this look like from the outside? The Empire eventually crumbled, and the people were very confused. They no longer had "daddy"—the Empire—to tell them who they were. There was a period of unrest and confusion. At this point, the Black League came out from the caverns and began to be the teachers. The Orion Christ ascended when it was time.

When Christ was born on Earth, it was hoped that the same thing would happen here as did in Orion. If it was successful in Orion, it had to be a success on Earth. Surprise! In the Orion system, they were all one species with one core ideology, for the most part. You are one species on Earth, but you have many extraterrestrial sources and you are much more individualistic than the Orions were. You, as a planetary species, have not yet learned how to shift like a group mind. The Orions could do this, and this is why it worked there. The reason it did not work here is that only some people got the message and shifted. Other people used Christ as a religious icon, missing the whole point and using it to fuel more war instead.

This was not the only time this type of shift was attempted. There was the life of Buddha. Some of the great sages and teachers from history represent attempts, but it hasn't been a success yet. One of the main reasons there were not as many bloody wars over the Buddha as there were over Christ is that in the East, the group-mind aspect of your mass consciousness is much more intact than it is in the West.

So you are here now with the challenge of shifting this and knowing that no one can "save" you. No one person can save you. What does this mean? You have to find the Christ inside of you—your *own* Christ.

You have to find your own Founder, your original Source. It has always been there. Let it begin to be born.

For those of you pursuing spiritual growth, this is not a foreign concept. But what about those of you with no background to even understand this concept? There is work to be done. From the perspective of the Founders, you are going to succeed. There is no question. It is just a matter of progressing through these amazing steps.

You were talking about the original Vegan mysticism and the cultures on Earth that were influenced by it. Were the Polynesians and Hawaiians influenced too?

We haven't yet gotten into the story of Lemuria, which massively influenced the Pacific cultures. We will talk about that soon. Some of those Pacific cultures have Vegan roots—like the Japanese—but they also have a Pleiadian overlay that is connected to the Lemurian evolutionary progression. We will shortly speak more about this.

You mentioned that some of our galactic mythology is played out in movies like Star Wars. Would you say movies like The Fifth Element and The Matrix are examples as well?

Oh yes!

Is George Lucas just tapped in to this? Are the moviemakers inspired in some way to help our awakening?

Oh yes. You can tell the difference between those who are simply inspired and those who, at some time and place, lived the same dynamics as those portrayed in a movie. Someone who has lived it has the stamina to see it through over a long period of time. They have a passion. George Lucas, Steven Spielberg, Frank Herbert, George Orwell, and many more have lived it and are writing from their archetypal memory, as well as their inspiration and passion.

Would we also be able to identify our own paths by what mythology we resonate with most?

Yes. These are wonderful mythologies to tell you where your connections are. It is very easy for someone outside of this type of belief system to say, "Oh, you are just fantasizing about *Star Wars.*" You *know* if it has a deep meaning for you. Listen to that. Listen to what aspect you resonate with. Is it the Jedi?

Yoda!

Yoda pushes a lot of buttons for many people. He is modeled after a great Black League teacher—one—who had the most compassion and gentleness. Most of them were not very gentle! They lived in warlike conditions. The Black League teacher that Yoda is modeled after had a great amount of compassion and was revered by thousands of people.

Was Rome a manifestation of the Orion Empire on Earth?

The Empire played itself out on Earth in many different ways—Rome, Nazi Germany, some aspects of your own government, some aspects of the European royalty, and so forth.

Since there was an electromagnetic net that kept souls in, would that impair the Orion Christ's ability to incarnate into the system?

Yes, initially it did impair the ability of the Christ to incarnate. But because the priests knew how to open the net, he was able to enter. The primary reason for the net was to prohibit escape. They were more interested in prohibiting escape than prohibiting entrance. They figured that if someone entered, they could trap them and thus have more people to control.

Do animals have souls?

Yes. They are, of course, created from the same energy as all of you. Imagine a human soul fragmenting more so that its energy source was not strong enough to maintain an ego. (You have to have a lot of energy to maintain an ego.) If a human fragmented more in its soul essence, it would technically become animalistic. That is not meant in a negative sense; it simply means "egoless." If you chose to become a dog in the next life, you would fragment into many dogs. The primary difference between the souls of animals and humans is the presence or absence of ego. Animals still communicate. They are still a part of all things as you are, but they just do not communicate in the same way or relate to reality in the same way because of a lack of ego.

What is very interesting is that many primates are beginning to develop ego. This means that they are beginning to evolve in a different way—into unification—by passing through an ego state before they pass beyond it into further integration.

I've read a lot on the Internet about the illuminati and the royal families on Earth and some of it is very dark. How do we integrate this unsettling information?

It is important to understand that, for the most part, those with the darkest intentions have them because they think they know what is "best." They think that if they were able to implement what is "best," everything would be wonderful. That is really where it is coming from on the deepest level. When the Lyrans first began their colonization, their ideology was to go out and conquer the universe as a means to get back to Source. This is exactly what some of the dark organizations feel. It is at the root of their agenda. The dark organizations are not just dark for the sake of darkness; they also have a spiritual component that they act out. They are continuing the Lyran ideology by forcing their view of reality onto other people as a way to return to Source.

Most of you can look at it objectively and see that it doesn't work that way. Integration will never happen through domination or manipulation. However, they have not let go of that belief system. They are still learning. Whenever you have polarity, there is a lesson to be learned. Because they believe in that way, all of you who are seeking to achieve your own sovereignty can use them as a mirrors to see the reflections of your disempowered selves. Without that, you might lose the direction you are moving in. You might not remember that you are here to achieve sovereignty.

There is a connotation that the Orion experience is negative, but I am starting to see this differently. I am seeing that this is all a part of who I am. When I see it that way, it loses its negativity and fear. I think this is how we can transmute it. The Lyrans, the Vegans—they are all part of our heritage and who we are!

Yes. Unfortunately, this presentation cannot go into so much depth that you could meet and talk to some of the representatives of the different cultures. There is an Orion priest named Akbar who has talked extensively in the past. When he comes through, the beauty and the love that you feel shows you the other side of the Orions. It shows you their passion and their deep spiritual commitment. So yes, your galactic heritage is deep; it has its shadows and valleys that give it dimension. It is not something that can be easily categorized into black and white.

We have been talking about the mythology of Star Wars. I was surprised how drawn I was to Darth Vader the last time I watched it, especially the scene where he is redeemed—he changes his mind and kills the emperor and then dies. The relationship between Darth Vader and Luke (his son) is very powerful to me. In the end, he had integrity and a warrior's code.

It is very interesting that many years after the original trilogy, you now get to see who Darth Vader really is. Many of you fell in love with him as a boy and watched how he turned to the "dark side." Your mythology will always parallel the mass consciousness. You are now getting ready to embrace your shadow self, to see that they can be loved. They are little children who want to be loved. This is a pivotal point that shows you that you are indeed on your way home. You cannot go home without embracing that darkness—the denied parts of yourself.

Will polarity be resolved on Earth, or does it have to be worked on nonphysically?

Earth is a nexus point for this resolution for a very specific reason. All the major players of your galactic family have influenced you genetically and culturally. Most of the major players have connections here. This is one of the most logical places for it to be resolved. Yes, it is being worked on nonphysically. However, it can never be resolved in the nonphysical realms. It must be resolved in a realm of fragmentation that is as far from Source as possible. It is kind of like stretching a rubber band. The moment that it stretches to its limits before it snaps back is where resolution must occur. It is up to you! The perspective from the nonphysical realms is that it happens simultaneously. There is no worry that you won't integrate, because you already have. Your unique perspective from a linear time framework drives you to put one step in front of another and complete it that way. But, it *has* already been done, and *will* be done, and *is* being done. So don't worry!

That does not mean to sit back and do nothing. Live your lives, live your passion, follow your truth, and heal yourselves. That will take care of it.

We talked about the whole point being to remember the oneness of Source and return home. When that happens, will the physical human race no longer exist, since it came out of the desire to experience separation?

Theoretically, the physical universe will no longer exist if all of you choose to go back to Source. But maybe some of the Founders who are stars and planets or some of the souls who are really enjoying it here might want to stay. If that happens, they will be here for the next group who want to experience the same polarity paradigm. This leads to another question. Let's say most of you want to go back. But some of the Founders in planet and star form—and some in body form—want to stay. A whole new group comes in. Does that mean the whole new group will actually experience true aliens waiting here? Yes.

If that is the case, then are there any true aliens in your reality now who are not part of your galactic family? Yes. Who are they? We will not get into that at this time.

You mentioned white holes and black holes earlier. Can you say more about them?

The only difference between a white hole and a black hole is what side of the phenomenon you are viewing. A white hole is an entrance point. A black hole is an exit point. It is simply a cycle, like a revolving door!

Earth, Lyrans, and Pleiadians

Let us bring it back to Earth, around the time the Vegans left because they lost the territory rights. The Lyrans began to colonize and spread out in the system. This was just around the end of the dinosaur era. The Lyrans had their heart set on some heavy-duty, massive genetic manipulation of the species that would later become primates on Earth. They felt these beings would be the most closely compatible with their consciousness. They thought they could create the perfect being that would help them return to Source. Here we go again!

Obviously these genetic projects would take a very long time to accomplish. But they had a lot of time because, unlike humans now, their life spans were very, very long. In the words of science-fiction author David Brin, galactic beings "think long thoughts." Long-term plans matter not at all, for time was different for these long-lived forefathers.

These Lyrans "thought long thoughts." The idea of engaging in a genetic project that would take hundreds of thousands of years was not a big deal to them. They viewed time in a different way. Thus they began their projects.

During this time, they were still sometimes living on Mars or Maldek in bases built there by the Vegans. They didn't really like it there all too much. The climate and atmosphere were not as suited to them as it was to the Vegans. They decided they would do whatever they could to live on Earth. Much time passed and groups broke off from the main established colonies and migrated to various parts of Earth. We are going to focus on one particular group for now.

There was a group that colonized the area that is now known as Scandinavia. The land masses were different then, but that is the general area. These Lyrans felt a very strong emotional affinity with Earth. They made their lives here because they loved it so much. They were involved with the genetic work just a little bit, but as time went on, they were not so interested. They were more interested in making Earth their home. Since they decided they wanted to settle on Earth, they felt it would be in their best interest to take some Earth genetics and incorporate them into themselves. They were still having a few problems adapting to the planet in regard to oxygen content, gravitation fields, and such. For this reason, they took small amounts of primate DNA and incorporated it into their successive generations. They were eventually able to adapt to Earth.

Time went on and their identity began to change. They were no longer Lyran. They became Earth-Lyran. That is how they saw themselves. (Notice "Earth" is first.) They began to identify with Earth much more than their Lyran roots.

Just about this time, there were conflicts going on with other extraterrestrial groups. There were lots of wars in the heavens and wars on Earth with different subgroups who wanted to conduct genetic engineering in different ways. It was becoming more and more difficult for them to live in peace without outside interference. It became unbearable. With a heavy heart, the Earth-Lyrans decided to leave Earth and go back out into space to find another star system that didn't have any claims. Their plan was to live, grow, and create a civilization that was free of polarity infighting.

Though the migration took quite a while, they eventually found themselves in the area you now know as the Pleiades. The seven stars that you see in the sky now are new stars. That particular area of space holds many stars in other frequencies, as well as stars even more distant than the ones you see. They colonized in that general area on older stars with systems that were already established. They found one particular planet that was very much like Earth; it was very green with lots of water and many resources. They made it their home.

As they developed their culture and bred and grew, they began to develop a whole new identity that would eventually be known as Pleiadian. Their roots, however, were as Earth-Lyrans. Many of the Pleiadians who interact with you now are literally your cousins, because genetically they share your DNA. Their interest in you is not just academic. It is also very emotionally based. Earth was their first home. They love Earth and have come back from time to time to interact with the different cultures that developed later on Earth. There is a very strong connection.

As the civilization in the Pleiades began to develop, other Lyran groups migrated and settled there as well. So in terms of genetic trees, you have Pleiadians whose genetic stock is Earth-Lyran and you have Pleiadians whose genetic stock is pure Lyran.

As the Pleiadians developed, they were a very spiritually connected civilization. They didn't share their Lyran forefathers' drive for conquest and colonization. In fact, though they had a little bit of Lyran in them (in terms of wanting to create their own society), they had some influence from Vegan mysticism as well. Some of their interactions with Vegan mystics in the past had seeded some very deep spiritual beliefs within them. They brought this spirituality to their new Pleiadian home.

Along the way, these new Pleiadians began to favor what you might call "light" over "darkness" (the shadow). Of course, most people do favor positivity over negativity. However, they began to deny their own darkness. They wouldn't look at it. The energy of dark and light within the humanoid psyche is an ebb and flow like ocean tides. Can you imagine trying to stop low tide and only focus on high tide? Can you imagine trying to force only a high tide environment? That was what they were attempting to do.

This created a huge imbalance within their psyches and the collective consciousness. Whenever there is an imbalance, the body or collective consciousness will always seek balance through whatever means available. The result was a plague that manifested itself through this Pleiadian system. The plague was similar to AIDS in that it hit the immune system. Their immune systems began to break down. Their normally vivacious, excited, passionate state gave way to weakness, lack of energy, and immune system failure. It began to get so bad that they pleaded with their scientists to find a cure. No one could.

Finally, they pleaded with their mystics who were well-versed in Vegan mysticism and spirituality. The mystics conducted what you might call a "vision quest" with prayer, chanting, and meditation. The mystics received a vision that totally explained what had happened: This plague was occurring because of rampant denial of darkness and the total imbalance within the psyche of the collective population. They found a way to work the population through ceremony, education, and retraining so they could begin to walk into their own darkness, face their own fear, and heal those parts of themselves. This experience for the Pleiadians was one of their most poignant memories. It's still very close to them because they realize how near they came to annihilation.

There was another historical event that was of major significance to the Pleiadians. At one point, the Pleiadians felt very "full of themselves." They wanted to go out into the universe and "save" everyone and go back to Source. They were displaying their Lyran roots quite strongly! They happened upon the Orion system in its darkest time. They saw what was going on with the Orion net keeping everyone encased, and they became incensed. They decided to march right in and liberate the Orion home worlds.

How do you think that turned out? The Orions retaliated by destroying an entire Pleiadian planet. Some of you may remember that in one of the *Star Wars* movies, the Empire destroys a planet that had a rebel base on it. It was a very small part of the movie. Do you remember the emotion when that planet was destroyed? That part of the movie was tapping into a memory.

Luckily, the Pleiadians learned their lesson after this planet was destroyed. They knew they could no longer meddle. They kept that charred and lifeless in its solar system. It is still there today. They kept it as a reminder of the folly of war, and as a reminder to maintain humility at all costs and never be arrogant.

That memory is one carried very deeply within the Pleiadian soul. Sometimes it is difficult for them to talk about it. Millions of people gave their lives so the civilization could learn that lesson.

Lemuria and Arcturus

Let's return to Earth now. There are so many aspects to the creation of the varied life on Earth because there are so many extraterrestrial species that influenced it. Let's move to the Pacific region, which would include southern Asia—India, Thailand, parts of Japan, Polynesia, Indonesia, and so on. This area in your mythology is known as Lemuria. Please keep in mind that we are skipping around in terms of planetary ownership and timelines. It is unavoidable for now.

During the time of Lemuria, there was a treaty. The planet was not just owned by the Lyran colonies—but there was a treaty that allowed for the interaction of many races. There was Lyran influence, Vegan influence, Sirian influence, Pleiadian influence, and more.

Right before the establishment of that colony of Lemuria, those in charge began to evaluate the galactic history up until that point. They saw that there hadn't really been much progress with anything. There was still conflict, war, and strife. What had really been accomplished?

So they decided that what was needed was Founder influence coming right from Source. They thought, "Let's see if we can seed this new colony with some Founder influence so that its foundation is one of being connected and remembering Source. Maybe this will stop conflict."

They put the call out, if you will: "What Founder wishes to help with this project?" The answer was that a Star Founder wanted to help. You know this Star Founder by the name of Arcturus. "All right, we will help," it said. Arcturus fragmented itself so that there was enough energy to incarnate. Well, in actuality it wasn't an incarnational process but more of a manifestation—a densification of the pure Arcturan Founder energy. Those were the first beings who established Lemuria in very ancient times.

They began to try to build a civilization in whatever way they could. Is there anything else happening on the planet at this time? Oh yes! On the other side of the planet, there are all of these genetic projects being done by Lyrans and Sirians (and others) who are still working on the creation of the "perfect" human using primate DNA. This was going on during the same time. The Pacific area was a bit more isolated at the time. Earth was very much a laboratory.

The Arcturan beings have influenced some of the Polynesian cultures, such as the Balinese, the early Indians, and the Indonesians, especially the Thai. The whole Polynesian chain was influenced, including Easter Island and what is now Hawaii.

So what is the nature of this Arcturan Founder energy? What is it like? This energy is fundamentally balanced male/female. It is emotionally balanced, which means that dark/light and love/fear and that whole dynamic are very equally balanced. It is extremely emotionally healing. So anyone coming in contact with an Arcturan energy and surrendering to it will be forced to move into a resonance with it. This would purge emotional blocks and bring forth healing.

Ideally then, this Arcturan energy could really be a wonderful foundation for a civilization. But of course they were aware that the civilization ultimately cannot be just Arcturan, because that is too integrated and will not achieve what they wish to do in this reality. Eventually they are going to have to fragment, and they knew that. For now they hoped to set the very strong base upon which they could then build their society.

Let us take a moment to tell you about the Arcturan energy as it relates to you as individuals. The Arcturan Founder has agreed to provide a very unique service for humans. Whenever you are born into this system or die and move out of this system, you pass through a tunnel between realities and you are connecting with the Arcturus energy. The best way to describe it is that Arcturus has embraced that tunnel and you are basically passing through the Arcturus energy when you are born or die. This serves to emotionally cleanse the person making the transition.

When babies come through, they have just come through the Arcturan gate. When souls who do not remain as astral, trapped entities leave through the Arcturus gate, they get cleansed as well. In a sense, Arcturus serves as like a black hole/white hole gate through which consciousness passes. This is the gift they have given to this reality.

For a period of time, the Lemurian civilization (in its early days) was very harmonious. There were no problems. But though we mean it in a very loving way, it was very sterile because it did not provide a challenge. The very early Lemurians took some of the ancient Vegan priesthood teachings because they had been adapted to Earth in the past. They began to implement them, because it became really obvious that Earth needed to begin to form its own identity. They figured that because the Vegans were the first ones here, they could use their mysticism practices, which had been around the longest.

After awhile, the other entities on the planet involved in the genetic engineering were watching the growing Lemurian culture and thought, "Hmm, that looks really idyllic. Maybe I'll take a vacation there!" There began to be more and more pressure for the rest of the planet to move into this Lemurian energy and interact with it. It was almost that the other civilizations saw Lemuria as a beautiful pond or fountain to drink from that would satiate their thirst. So you can see where this is going!

The other groups on the planet began to fight over who would control this paradise—the same story! Just about this time, these Arcturan beings began to go into hiding. At that time, hiding meant going into lava caves in Polynesia that went deep into Earth; some began or ended up in Peru, Chile, Bolivia, western North America, Asia, or Indonesia.

These Arcturan beings did not want to participate in the control battles in Lemuria but they were not going to give up on their agreement to come to Earth and assist. Thus they simply lived underground and became the caretakers of the planet's energy—the energy of the mass consciousness. They made themselves available to assist with emotional healing or any other kind of healing for those who were sensitive enough to perceive their energy and ask for help. They would never impose their help without being asked.

At this point, you had a migration into Lemuria by the other beings on the planet. This was a hodgepodge: Lyrans, Vegans, Sirians, Pleiadians, and other assorted characters. They began to take over the civilization and attempt to emulate how the Lemurians lived, but of course they never really had the same energy behind their actions as the Lemurians did.

Atlantis

Around this time, in the later days of Lemuria, you had another growing civilization on the other side of the world that you know of as Atlantis. It was also a melting pot of various different species. But rather than the Lemurian ideology of getting back to Source and the spiritual pursuits, the Atlantean ideology was basically the same as the Lyran—technological development, expansion out into space, and conquest.

This expansiveness is not necessarily negative when it is done from a place of balance. For a while Atlantis was in balance, because it did produce some very wonderful technologies that were very healing and beneficial to the people. But it began to be tainted once the Orion migration started. When we say the "Orion migration," we are referring to what was mentioned earlier. Some of the priests would open holes in the Orion net, go through them, and come to Earth. They would come to Atlantis because it was more familiar to them.

The Empire would pursue them through the net into Atlantis, and the whole dynamic was created over again.

You can see the polarity dynamic being set up again. We do not have to tell you what happened with Atlantis, because you know the story. It basically tore itself apart because of the battle of polarities. It also tore apart Lemuria for the most part. Once Atlantis expanded to its capacity, it wanted to obtain other lands. Lemuria fell very easily because it wasn't focused on war.

The fall of Atlantis and Lemuria all occurred during a period of time when there was a tremendous amount of Earth changes—what you might call a polar shift. So this actually facilitated the ending of those eras. But there were still areas on Earth engaging in genetic experiments to create the perfect human. Now get ready for some convolution of time and space—more so than we've already given you!

Some of the Founders (the architects) who were watching over this experiment began to see that this wasn't going to work. They began to run a future projection, much like one would run a mathematical projection. They saw that Earth was not going to survive. They felt they must do something to change a variable that would set the Earth on another path. They made a radical decision.

The Zeta Reticuli

From the Founders' level of consciousness, it is no big deal to move through time. They connected with future probabilities to find a species that could give them some guidance. They found the species you now know as the Zeta Reticuli, or the "Grays" as some of you call them. These beings exist in a one-mind culture. For those of you *Star Trek* fans, they are kind of like the Borg, but without all the negative manifestations. They are a simple, one-minded, unified field consciousness in many bodies.

Forget what you think you know about the Zetas. We are not talking about what you read in the fear-producing literature. The Zetas lent some DNA to the Founders and said, "Use this DNA. Go back and create a new timeline for Earth. Do this by creating a new Earth species."

Up until this point, around the time of Lemuria and Atlantis, the only species that were really interacting on Earth were the Lyrans, (who were somewhat more Caucasian) and the Vegans (who were somewhat more darker-skinned). Even in the genetic experiments using the primate DNA, they were modeling these new beings in their own image. They weren't so much making a new species as they were making copies of themselves. The Zetas said, "No. You must make a *new* species. Here is how to do it, and the reason you need to do it is because the variable of unified mind must be instilled into the mass consciousness of Earth, or it will not survive."

The Role of Asia

So the Founders went back into the continent of Asia and began working on a new genetic project using the DNA from the Zeta Reticuli to create what is now the Asian race. We know this is somewhat out there. But right now on your planet, you have East and West. If you look at the ideologies of the two, there are some very strong polarities. Now, in this time frame on Earth, you are finding that the East and West are beginning to meet and blend. Given the opportunity to do so, what the Founders felt was that this would calm the individualistic nature of the planet and eventually begin to teach all beings to live from the point of view of a group mind. (We don't mean being group mind like a bunch of zombies! This would simply enable you to live within unity and diversity simultaneously. There is the paradox.)

These genetic experiments in Asia were very protected and well-guarded. Pretty soon they had prototypes of what you would now call an Asian race. They scattered them throughout Asia.

This is something that myself (Germane) and Sasha (a Pleiadian) have discussed with groups in Japan a lot. We've taken groups in Japan to some of the sites where the prototypes were kept and educated. Some of this information is available on tape. These Asian prototypes were the turning point in setting your world on its course toward integration.

Once the genetic bodies were created and began procreating, some of the key prototypes were kept in educational facilities. They were educated in Vegan mysticism and also in some Pleiadian spiritual practices that are very feminine in nature. The Asian culture was ideologically influenced by an underlying Arcturan energy but also by Vegan mysticism and Pleiadian spirituality.

The prototypes were taught about consciousness, unified fields, and the mind/body connection. They were taught that the human was a holistic unit rather than a collection of organs, skin, and bones. They felt that these Asian prototypes had to be taught this immediately before they were imprinted with other belief systems that would be passed genetically into their offspring. This was very intense training in Vegan mysticism. Once the prototypes graduated—and there was indeed a graduation vision quest and ceremony—they were then allowed to go out, reproduce, and seed the whole area of Asia and some parts of Polynesia and Indonesia.

In a sense, this was done under the nose of the rest of the planet. The other cultures were so absorbed with their own prototype projects that they didn't pay much attention and didn't think it would be much of a success anyway. Pretty soon the Vegan teachings, as carried in these early Asian prototypes, began to spread and affect the tapestry of the mass consciousness itself, literally changing the course of Earth's journey. We cannot really stress this enough. If it wasn't for those Zetas and the Founders who brought back the DNA and implemented this, we don't think you would have made it this far. There would have been too much individualism and polarity.

Now you can see why there is such a difference between the teachings of the East and the teachings of the West—though there are indeed some parallels and connections between them. There has always been a feeling in the belief system of the West that the East has been hiding something, or that there are some great secrets there. That is true—there are. It isn't just in the wisdom taught to the Asian prototypes; remember that the Arcturian Founders who went underground are still there. They are still the caretakers. They are the beings you refer to now as the Inner Earth beings. They are very old; they have been here a very long time.

During the destruction of Atlantis, there were some very powerful and positive priests in Atlantis—and others from all over the world—who needed to go underground to preserve the knowledge they had gained thus far on the planet. It was these Inner Earth beings, the Arcturan beings, who housed them and made sure they were all right. Even in this time now, they still hold some of the most sacred teachings on Earth. These have not yet been given to the public freely because of what would happen if they were. They are still caretaking this. So you have some very powerful guardians who are looking out for you and the best interests of the planet. They are not going anywhere, because they take their commitment very seriously.

The Zeta Reticuli Beginnings

Let's go back in time. We were talking about the Vegans and their early development. There was a group of Vegans who split off from one of the groups and developed their own colonies and their own planetary systems. Over time, they found themselves falling in line with the Lyran ideology. They somehow took a turn and began to become very technologically focused. They lost their connection to their planet and the memories of where they came from. They turned to science and technology for their solace, feeling that they could control their universe.

Eventually they polluted their planet, which polluted their people, who became very ill. They let their passions rule and destroy them. They eventually had a civilization on the brink of destruction. Most of the females and males could not reproduce due to the poisons they had taken into their bodies, among other reasons. They knew that they had to do something very dramatic or they wouldn't make it. So what did they do?

They realized their emotions were at the root of their situation. They took all that they had learned about genetic engineering and said, "We are going to engineer ourselves to live without emotions. That will solve the problem." They did this. They began repopulating themselves through the laboratory. Of course they did not get any less toxic. It did not help their planet, which got so bad that they had to live underground. They continued with the genetic tinkering. They no longer had emotional bodies and, of course, became very imbalanced.

Thousands of years went by and they realized they needed help. They had taken a wrong turn. They had done the wrong thing to heal themselves. They were at a total loss as to how to repair the damage. (We are making this story very brief. There are longer versions in the book *Visitors from Within*.) Eventually, it came down to finding another source of genetic material in order to survive. They wanted to make the journey back to Source and thought they had the answer of how to get back. But it wasn't the answer.

Their answer was to find another species with which they had a connection—a species that would volunteer to help them reclaim what they had lost so they could get back onto the path of reintegration with Source. Guess who volunteered? Earth humans.

These beings who were in trouble are called the Zeta Reticuli, or Grays. Again, forget everything you have read that is fear-based. That doesn't come into the story. Some of that information is disinformation and convolution. Think only of the story we are telling you now instead.

What did the Zetas give in return for this assistance? Well, one thing they gave—as we stated earlier—was some of the genetic material, along with guidance about one-mindedness that helped to create the Asian race to ultimately save Earth. Another thing is that through the interaction of two species that in some ways are very much at the opposite ends of the spectrum, each species can learn about fear and love. A human can look at a Zeta and a Zeta can look at a human; each can see its opposite self and walk through that fear. The Zetas can learn about individuality. Humans can learn about unification. Both will be served. In addition, some very generous Earth beings offered their own DNA to help create a new species that is a cross between Zeta and human.

Again, this sounds like an old story. Here we go again with another new species—is this one going to make it? But this species, a combination of you and them, has a great promise of survival—not just because of the genetic tinkering, but because of the intent behind it. This intent is not to make the perfect human, just like everyone else wanted to do. The intent is to face the shadow, the opposite self—to love it, embrace it, and become it—therefore paving the path to reintegration into Source.

You have all these dramas going on simultaneously. It is enough to give you a headache! There is really no need to worry about any one of them. Just know that all of this is going on simultaneously. It is a grand dance, like a choreographed ballet. And even though at times it may seem perilous, we are certain that eventually the outcome will be reintegration.

You were talking about how the Vegans ended up destroying themselves by engineering themselves to have no emotion, but then you started talking about the Zetas. What is the relationship between them?

The Vegan culture was the genetic source of the Zetas. In this presentation we have shown how different species migrated and became other species throughout time. An offshoot of the Vegans eventually became the Zetas.

What is left of the Vegans?

There aren't many Vegans left in their original form. There are many cultures that are remnants of Vega—like Altair, for instance. However the identity of Vegans as it existed millennia ago does not exist in the same way now. It is more that the Vegan ideology still exists as it is embodied within other cultures now.

Do Arcturians live underground at Mount Shasta?

Yes. Regarding the Arcturan Founders who have taken bodily form, we need to make clear that there are other Star Founders on the planet who have also served as caretakers. We chose to use Arcturus because they are a major influence.

What was Christ's influence?

Oh boy, this leads us into a messy area! He had a strong Arcturan influence: balance. Throughout time, the powers that be—those running the genetic projects) always tried to create the perfect being. In the case of Christ and other well-known entities on your world, there was an attempt at joining what might be called two royal houses. As you know, an alliance is formed when you join two royal houses, and it is hoped that both can benefit from the joining. Christ represented a genetic cross. At the time of Christ, the royal houses were no longer Lyra and Vega; it was Lyra and Sirius. (The Vegans who were connected directly to Earth had migrated to Sirius and thus identified themselves as Sirians.) At that point, the Sirians were the real genetic engineers. They were very adept.

Christ was an attempt at joining two royal star houses in the hope that peace could be brought. This was also an attempt to create the perfect human being. It was hoped that Christ would reproduce and insert a cross of genetics into the gene pool on Earth. He did reproduce, and his decendents became the Merovingian line. You find their trail in history throughout Europe. Remember that it was rumored Princess Diana was of Merovingian blood; thus her child who will be king someday, will be Merovingian. Even in Japan there is a place called the grave of Christ. It is believed that Christ came to this village in Northern Japan after his so-called crucifixion. He settled here, had a family, and eventually died.

So Christ's genetics are indeed in the gene pool of your planet. Anything in the gene pool is in the grid of mass consciousness, and thus a part of you as well. If there is one mutation in the gene pool on Earth, the entire gene pool will change, due to the holographic principle.

Is that how the genetic engineers seeded Earth?

Partially. At the very beginning, they were all working on individual projects. The genetic engineering in Africa led to the creation of the African races. Genetic engineering in Asia led to the Asian races, of course. In the Americas, it led to the Native American races. Genetic engineering in Europe led to the Caucasian races, and so on. At first these were all individual projects but eventually there started to be crossbreeding. The changes began happening not just on the surface but within the mass consciousness as well. Even right now, as an example, if you suddenly took all the blacks and brought them to Africa and all the Asians and brought them to Asia, separating people by region, those lines of separation wouldn't work. You are already changed as a whole. You can be separated by artificial boundaries, but it doesn't matter because your identity is as one people. You *have* to learn to live together. When you all learn to coexist in peace, you are really only making peace with other aspects of yourself.

Can you talk about the capstone of the pyramid? I heard it is connected to Venus, Sirius, and Orion energy.

First of all, Venus is a gate for Sirius energy as well as Pleiadian energy. Venus is probably one of the primary gates in your solar system for galactic energy. Regarding Egypt, perhaps you are aware of some of the work of scientists who have researched the pyramids on the Giza plateau and other temples. These pyramids are exact scale replicas of the Orion constellation. Most of you know that the pyramids are certainly much older than archaeologists are saying they are. When these temples were set up in the pattern of Orion, it was a reminder to anyone coming to this planet—(and to yourselves)—that the main theme you are working on is the integration of polarity. It also reminds you that the main star connection you are healing is Orion.

When we spoke about the Orion net, we talked about how the priests would migrate and come to Earth. Some of the Orion gates they passed through on Earth are in the Middle East. Thus it is no coincidence that Orion is the whole theme over Egypt. Osiris had a huge Orion connection. The precursor to the Egyptian gods—(the Sumerians)—had huge Orion, Sirius, and Lyra connections as well.

There are other places on Earth where pyramid configurations mirror the Orion constellation. In the southwest, the city of Phoenix has it too—but those temples are so ancient that their remnants are under the city at this point. There are other areas in the Southwestern United States. Areas in Mongolia are connected to Orion as well. The Orion energy has basically been stamped on this planet. This is what you cannot escape from. You have to heal this. This is a reminder that you are not going anywhere until those wounds are healed.

So the Orion thing is what we see it to be. One thing I learned from this session is that it is helpful and it is in us to be healed. We can look at this differently. It doesn't have to have an outcast energy. We don't have to get rid of it. I need to just transmute all this fear about Orion into love.

Yes. We'll tell you a secret. Sometimes people have asked us, "Germane, if you could categorize your energy, what would it be?" The best way we can describe our matrix of consciousness is that we would call ourselves the "Orion light." This does not mean polarized light— the opposite of dark. If you were to take the entire Orion drama and the way it played out even on other worlds, entirely integrated and healed, it would be the Orion light. That is all of *you* as well. You *are* this. We are not that scary, we hope!

Germane, is there any way for you to give us a glimpse of what we look like to you? What do we really look like?

We see you with two arms, two legs, and a head, but as lightbeings who are just moving in fluid light. Your head is not round, but more oval. That is how we see you. We don't really see you as individuals. We can see that there are different beings in the room. We don't *see* your individual differences per se, but you *feel* different to us. That is the best way to describe it. Sorry for being so vague!

Just to clarify, you are saying that right now on Earth there aren't beings who are specifically Vegan, Orion, or Lyran, right? Are you saying that we have all become sort of one species holographically? We are one species now? We are Earth humans and each one of us has all of this inside of us? Maybe someone has more Lyra than Vega, but we are truly Earthlings?

Yes, absolutely. There are still Pleiadians, Arcturians, Sirians, and so forth, out there. On your world, however, you have literally created a new species of unification from your galactic family. Initially, genetic crossbreeding is important because of a need to change the gene pool, but continued crossbreeding is not important. You could stop crossbreeding now, because you have already set this species integration in motion.

Well the human genome right now is very uniform. You can't look at it and see any differences except for the specific orientations of the amino acids. But human beings are human beings.

Yes, yes. In the past—such as during the genetic projects—if you were to examine those new humans in Africa, Europe, and Asia, they would seem as if they were different species, though closely related. It is not that way any more.

How does Egypt carry our memories as a planet, and how do Atlantis and Lemuria fit into that?

Most of the Egyptian gods and most of the Egyptian myths—for instance the story of Osiris and Isis—are actually Egyptian versions of the memories of an older culture. What you know of Egyptian mythology is actually close to Mesopotamia—Babylon, Sumeria, and even earlier cultures. That is where these myths were created. They were passed through the generations, through different civilizations, and each civilization adapted them as their own. So this idea of Osiris being chopped up is a metaphor but has its roots in an older culture. Even the being Kwan Yin has parallels with Inanna, Isis, and so on. You have been carrying the same myths and repackaging them, depending on the culture. This has kept your memory alive. A lot of these memories come from even more ancient times, those of Atlantis and Lemuria. There are much more ancient cultures that are the source or root of many of these myths. And for the newer civilizations—like ancient Greece—that have their own myths, many of their dramas adhere to the archetypes played out in earlier civilizations.

Can you talk about Nibiru?

Not much at this time, but the writings that you have talk about Nibiru being in an elliptical orbit that comes through your solar system every 3,600 years. We would agree with that, but we would expand on it and say that the planet Nibiru is also part of the Sirius system, though it may be part of your solar system for a temporary period of time. You and the Sirius system are very strongly connected. If you were out in Lyra or somewhere else in space, looking in your telescope toward this part of the galaxy, you would most likely think that Sirius, Sol (Earth's sun), and Vega are a part of the same constellation or even system. From *your* perspective, Vega is in the Lyran system. But from somewhere out in space, it would look more like it is part of your system because it is so close.

Yes, Sirius is about eight light-years from Earth and Vega is about fourteen. So from space, it might look like three stars close together. Also, can I ask a question about Mars and what is now the asteroid belt (Maldek)? You said there was a planet there. Are there remains of the former colonization activity on Mars? Can we discover it when we go there?

Yes, yes. Some of it has already been discovered. As for the asteroid belt, there were several different things that caused the destruction of that planet. One was that the society living there was degenerating—lots of war. There was an external cataclysm, or impact, and there was also some punishment. There was a skirmish and someone "out there" felt that Maldek was expendable. It was helped along in its destruction.

We know there is some information that Earth was pulled from Taimat, another planetary body. Earth is younger than some of the other planets like Mars. It was formed later by a cataclysm. When the solar system was first created, there were only four large planets. Fragmentation occurred through various events, creating even more planets. This is very natural.

Are we correct in thinking that the beings were first on Maldek, then Mars, and from there they migrated to Earth?

Well, Maldek and Mars were originally colonized by the Vegans in *very* ancient days. For a period of time, there was simultaneous colonization of both.

I heard that there are some Pleiadians and Orions still living on Mars and controlling Earth's events. Is this true?

Not to the extent that the rumors would like you to think. There is definitely an influence surrounding Mars. We've not really been allowed to talk about this. We don't mean that someone isn't allowing it; it is more that, from a bird's-eye perspective, we can sense what serves you and what doesn't. There is a faction that believes it owns Mars, and there have been some incidents—like Phobos, the Earth probe that was destroyed when it went to Mars—that resulted from these groups believing they own Mars. Right now, Mars is in dispute. With humans developing rudimentary space travel, Earth is becoming another faction that must be dealt with. Those in the know in your government understand that something is going on, and they are not pushing expeditions to Mars at this time.

So in numbers, are you talking a thousand or less?

Less.

Are they physically incarnated there?

Not incarnated in terms of "born" there. It is more like being temporarily housed there in physical bodies, but not what you know to be third-dimensional. They are a slightly different frequency. Realities might not align between the two of you, but you can still influence each other energetically.

Are they negatives and are they influencing Earth?

It is not our perspective to ever label anyone negative. That is a polarity. The very thing we are attempting to communicate with you today is that it is a lot different than that. We will not confirm that. But what we will say is that there are always attempts by various groups to exert their influence. There is a group associated with Mars attempting to influence and control—whether this makes them negative is a value judgment that we cannot make. Each of you often tries to exert your control on others too. That doesn't mean you are negative either.

What about the face on Mars? Is it really a face?

It performs the same function as the overlay of Orion in the Giza plateau. It is a reminder. Just like any good Rorschach test, what you see in it is what you need to see.

Can you tell us how many planets are populated? Maybe not just in our dimension, but how many are populated in some way throughout all the dimensions?

Hmm. "Populated." You would have to define "populated."

Dense and physical beings.

With a few exceptions, just about every planet has consciousness associated with it. Remember what we said at the very beginning—the planets and the stars are the Founders. For example, in the case of the Pleiadian planet that was destroyed and left there as a reminder, there is no consciousness associated with it and that was deliberate. Those who see it can really feel the deadness and the folly of war. Most have consciousness associated with them. Some have more individualized consciousness, like Earth. Planets like Neptune, have much more nonphysical consciousness associated with them. It really depends on the planet.

What about our Moon?

To some degree—and you might find this answer shocking—the Moon has very little consciousness associated with it. But let us explain. In civilizations that have trouble getting in touch with and validating their own darkness, people need symbols to remind them. The Moon has always been associated with the esoteric—going within and making spiritual journeys. In females, you have the moon time—a time when you go within. When you are out in the desert or forest communing with the Moon and doing sacred work, you are going within. We do not mean to imply the Moon is barren and has no consciousness. The consciousness associated with the Moon is not meant to give you something, but to remind you of something. Like the tide, it can help pull the darkness out of you. The Moon has cycles where it is visible and not visible that connect it with the tides. It is literally responsible not just for the tidal flow but for providing an energetic flow for each of you to feel your power. You feel this power in a masculine way when the Moon is full and waxing and feel your feminine power when the Moon is waning. This provides the frequency to remind you of the flow of the universe. Its purpose is not like the Founder associated with Venus. It is very different. It is for a *very* specific purpose that helps each of you maintain your connections.

What about the Founder that is associated with our sun, Sol?

He is so often overlooked. He has to have a great sense of humor! I will have a conversation with him, just a moment. [Pause.] He says that his consciousness "piggybacked" on the Founder who first manifested in the Lyran system as one of the first suns. When we say "piggybacked," we mean he didn't actively participate but was there in energy. He also piggybacked on the suns of several civilizations of Vega before Sol was born. The reason for this was that Sol needed to watch the very beginnings of humanoid life so that when he became his own sun, he would have wisdom to help guide you through the integration of polarity. He wanted to see your beginnings. From the very beginning, he knew he would eventually be the sun—Sol—who would create the solar system that would help the integration of the whole galactic family. Even though the sun is not as old as others in this incarnation, he has much experience and wisdom behind him.

I have a few questions about religion or spirituality. The desire for these ancient ET civilizations has been to return to Source. In the Eastern traditions, there are practices that help people return to that consciousness and experience themselves as infinite and eternal. But the return to Source is really done in consciousness, not in physical experience. That is available to all of us at any time?

Yes! The challenge has been the distraction of physicality. Obviously, when you accomplish something through great challenges, that's when you really learn it. The belief has been to take yourself far away from the thing in order to know the thing. Therein lies the paradox. So yes, it is really all up to you. If any of you could truly know the true consciousness and know how to put that knowingness into practice while totally ignoring the distractions, you could probably ascend immediately. There would be no reason to be here.

The irony is that the more you may want to ascend, the more you actually have to stay! When you love being here and you roll in the earth and you are fully here . . . you go!

Is it possible to maintain that connection and always know my true self, yet stay here and play?

Yes! Everything is possible.

Epilogue

This state of remembering our True Selves or our infinite awareness, has been a quest of spiritual seekers since before recorded history. Our extraterrestrial forefathers are no exception. Through their journeys away from Source and into the distraction of physical reality and all of its dramas, they often forgot their true nature as infinite consciousness. But somehow their inner drive to reunify and break the illusion of the temporary experience of physical reality kept them moving forward, with integration as the eventual result.

Today, we *are* our forefathers. We forge ahead into the unknown with a nagging emptiness that keeps us searching beyond religion and New Age explorations into a deeper place of authenticity and knowingness. In this still, silent place, we learn to differentiate between the distractions, opinions, and dramas of the ego (including the seduction of illusory physical reality), and the realm of paradoxical emptiness and fullness in which our true awareness abides.

Through the authentic practices of esoteric spirituality on Earth—which was very much influenced by Vegan mysticism—the ancients created many road maps that point the way home; they have been left to us as the most valuable of gifts. One of the most profound Vedic road maps, *The Yoga Sutras of Patanjali*, points out the last of the challenges in our awakening—our ability to differentiate between what is truly real and what is not. This simplified interpretation of two sutras makes this challenge clear:

II.17: *The cause of our suffering is our inability to differentiate between what is the truth (the one who perceives, that is, the eternal awareness) and what appears to be the truth (the one that is perceived by eternal awareness, that is, the human mind).*

II.23: *The inability to differentiate between the temporary, fluctuating mind and our True Self (eternal awareness) is the cause of our suffering. Yet this suffering provides us with the opportunity to learn differentiation and grow from it by understanding the true nature of both mind and eternal awareness.*

As awareness grows on Earth—which is happening at a very rapid rate—we facilitate the reunification not only of our galactic family but with Source itself, as our extraterrestrial forefathers intended. One step at a time, with open hearts and minds, we take this journey together. ॐ

Glossary of Terms

abductions: From the point of view of an abductee, this is the unwilling detainment by various extraterrestrial groups for the purposes of: (1) study; (2) genetic sampling; (3) tracking of genetic family histories; (4) maintaining and developing hybridization programs; (5) human maternal response observation; (6) observation of neurological responses to emotional stimuli; (7) communication; and other purposes including (8) the instillment of fear and terror, which is believed by the negatively oriented extraterrestrials to halt the development or acceleration of the abductees and of the mass consciousness. Listed are some groups involved in abductions and their primary reasons for interaction.

Zeta Reticuli: #1, 2, 3, 4, 5, 6, 7
Physical Sirians (negative): #1, 2, 3, 8
Pleiadians: #1, 3, 6, 7
Grays: #8
Physical Orions (negative): #8

Adam: This is the label given to the first stable prototype model of *Homo sapiens*. "Adam" comes from the Hebrew "Adama," meaning "created of the Earth's soil," thus "Earthling." In Sumerian the word is "Adapa," meaning "model man."

All That Is: This is a term that many use in place of "God" or the "Creator," because it includes the observer as part of the Creator.

Altair: Altair, whose civilization was colonized from Vega, lies 15.2 light-yearss from Earth. Altair's magnitude is 1.3 and its color pale yellow. The Altair civilization is quiet and contemplative, given to peaceful philosophic orientation. They are not currently involved in space exploration.

Andromeda: Andromeda is a large spiral galaxy and is the closest to the Milky Way at a distance of 2.2 million light-years. The nature of the Andromeda realm is abstract and fluid. A dimensional doorway exists in our nearby galactic neighborhood as a bridge to the Andromeda energy. This bridge/doorway is the star Antares.

angels/angelic kingdom: Existing within the realms of fifth and sixth density, the angelic kingdom has interacted with Earth through various means. These include spirit-guide manifestation, visions, inspiration, channeling, and telepathic communication. Energies appearing as angels are frequently from the Arcturus realm.

Antares: Lying in the Scorpius constellation, Antares is considered a binary star of fiery red and emerald green. Antares is the interdimensional bridge to Andromeda from our galaxy. Some souls, during physical incarnation, choose to pass through the Antares gateway to reactivate soul memory.

Anubis: In ancient Egypt, Anubis was considered a guide of the underworld. His usual depicted form was that of a crouching desert dog or jackal. He was known to lead souls through the astral (as in dream state) as well as to Amenti, or land of the dead. It is interesting how the prefix "an" in both Sumerian and Egyptian means "of Heaven." Anubis (Anpu in Egyptian) and Anu (Sumerian) both possessed the symbology of the jackal or dog, suggesting a direct connection to the Dog Star Sirius.

Apex Planet, Apexians: The Apex planet was one of the first developed societies in the Lyran star group. After its planetary catastrophe, the Apex planet was shifted dimensionally into another region of space-time. The Apexians eventually became the race of the Zeta Reticuli.

Some theorize that the Apex planet is really a parallel reality of Earth—one in which we never balance our technological development with our spiritual. If this is the case, then the Zeta Reticuli visitors may in fact be our own future selves interacting with our past selves.

archetype: The Living Webster Encyclopedic Dictionary defines archetype as "model or first form; the original pattern after which a thing is made or to which it corresponds." This definition suggests that all of our archetypal ideas are inherent patterns (dating from the birth of galactic humanity) that continue to evolve. New symbols of these patterns are being found, but the innate properties are the same.

Arcturus: Arcturus is seen as a golden yellow star with a magnitude of 0.3. Its energy works with humanity as an emotional and spiritual healer. It is also an energy gateway through which humans pass during death and birth. It functions as a way station for nonphysical consciousness to become accustomed to physicality.

Arcturus/Sirius Matrix: The combined energies of Arcturus and Sirius provide a balance of physical, emotional, and spiritual healing. This matrix has been tapped into by humanity since its inception and has been known through many archetypal ideas.

Association of Worlds: The Association is a group of physical and nonphysical beings from many realms who come together for a number of purposes. Some have called them a galactic confederation or federation. There is no hierarchical structure or authority inherent in the Association. The primary purposes for their interactions with Earth are: (1) to gently nudge humanity toward a greater awareness of itself and its place within the Association and (2) to prevent a critical number of nuclear explosions on Earth, which can cause a rip in the fabric of space-time, affecting the galactic neighborhood. They have absolutely no intention of evacuating anyone from Earth under any conditions. They understand the absolute necessity for the human race to become responsible for itself.

Atlantis: This was the combined extraterrestrial/human cultural period prior to the flood. The flood occurred in approximately 11,000 B.C.

Australopithecus: This term denotes any hominid of the extinct genus *Australopithecus* of the Pleistocene epoch. Advanced *Australopithecus* is the first being considered to be truly humanlike, existing some 2 million years ago.

bipedal: Any being possessing two feet can be considered bipedal.

black hole: A star becomes a black hole when it collapses and reaches such a high density that its gravitational field exceeds the escape velocity of even light photons. Astronomers theorize that a change in space-time occurs. This creates many probabilities, including (1) entrance and exit points to other dimensional realities, (2) birthplaces of future stars, (3) an ability to harness the powers of time travel, and (4) an entrance into an antimatter universe.

Black League: The Black League was an organizational resistance pattern developed during the Orion conflicts to counter the efforts of the Orion Empire, which was attempting physical and spiritual domination of the entire region. The Black League manifested not only as underground paramilitary resistance organizations but as a spiritual and philosophical orientation that manifested in many forms. These patterns have attempted balance in other planetary systems and are presently playing out on Earth through the human reincarnational cycle.

cetaceans: Cetaceans are marine mammals of the order "cetacea" which include whales, dolphins, and porpoises. Cetaceans possess consciousness of the same type as humans (but oriented more within fourth density), and are considered by extraterrestrials to be water humans.

channeling: Channeling is the process of receiving communication from an infinite number of dimensional realities. This communication can be expressed via writing, verbal relay, artwork, music composition, and any creative expression.

cherubim: The most ancient references concerning forms of cherubim (in the Akkadian and Sumerian records) describe a mechanical security device (i.e., robot) that was used to secure the highly sensitive areas of the gods to which humans were denied access. This idea later evolved into a more abstract and spiritual one, displayed in the archetypal manifestation of a winged celestial figure who guards sacred places and who is a servant of God.

Christ consciousness: The Christ consciousness is the aspect of a mass consciousness that recognizes itself as a single being. This can be equated with a sixth-density vibration. The term "Christ" is often misleading. Like Christ or Buddha, it is a level of consciousness without duality and can be labeled as sixth density, or Christ consciousness.

cloning: Cloning is an asexual method for reproduction that uses an original seed or genetic stock for replication.

consciousness: Consciousness is the underlying binding force of all creation. It exists in infinite manifestations and may defy definition.

Cro-Magnon: Cro-Magnon was a group of tall, erect, prehistoric people who used bone and stone implements. Thirty-five thousand years ago this new race of beings (identified with the larger type *Homo sapiens*, or thinking man) appeared seemingly out of nowhere and coexisted for a period of time with the dying race of the Neanderthal.

crystal skull: Found in southern Mexico, the skull is carved out of crystal in the shape of a human cranium. The most well-known skull is the Anna Mitchell-Hedges skull. Many claim to have mystical or paranormal experiences when they are in the skull's presence.

DAL: Referred to in the contact material from Billy Meier, the DALs are an interdimensional humanoid species who act as mentors for the Pleiadians.

density: Density denotes a vibrational frequency and not a location, which the term "dimension" implies. The density structure of this reality is primarily expressed in seven levels, though each level has sublevels within it. The density scale is a model used to communicate one's perception of orientation in relation to other realities.

devic: In Sanskrit, deva means a god or divinity; one of an order of good spirits. In Western mysticism, the devic energy is the spirit consciousness of mineral, plant, animal, and more subtle forms such as fairies.

Dimension: Dimension refers to one's location in space-time rather than a person's vibrational frequency (density). *Webster's* defines "dimension" as: "Magnitude measured in a particular direction, specifically length, breadth, thickness, or time." There are an infinite number of dimensions existing within a given density or vibrational frequency.

Dimensional Infusion: God—The Whole, All That Is—became curious about the idea of separation and unknowing and created a realm in which to explore those ideas. This was achieved by creating the boundaries of dimension. One may equate the Dimensional Infusion with the process of creation itself.

DNA: DNA is the abbreviation for deoxyribonucleic acid, which is a compound found in chromosomes and consists of a long-chain molecule comprising many repeated and varied combinations of four nucleotides, one of which is the sugar deoxyribose; subdivisions of the molecule are believed to be the genes. DNA is the major repository of genetic information.

Dogon: The Dogon people are an African tribe living in the Mali Republic (western Africa) near Timbuktu, thought to have migrated from Egypt. For many generations they have possessed a knowledge of advanced astrophysics concerning the Sirius star system that they claim was given to them by beings from that system.

Easter Island: Easter Island is located in the Pacific between Chile and French Polynesia and is known for the mysterious statues of humanoid beings left scattered throughout the island. Author Lyssa Royal has had direct experience of electromagnetic anomalies and UFO activity on this island.

ego: Ego is the "I" or self as distinguished from the selves of others. It is that part of the psyche that is conscious in physical reality and acts as the mediator between inner and outer worlds.

Enki: In Sumerian, Enki means "Lord of Earth" and he is considered to be the one who imparts the knowledge of civilization to humankind. He was also known to the Babylonians as "Oannes," and to the Egyptians as "Ptah." He was the god of wisdom and knowledge, and throughout time his symbol has been the snake. According to the Sumerian texts, Enki was the one who instructed Noah to build an ark so humanity could be saved. This was in direct defiance of the orders of Enlil, who desired the destruction of humanity.

Enlil: In Sumerian, Enlil means "Lord of the Air" and he was considered to be the chief of all the lands. The Sumerians considered him to be supreme. Enki and Enlil were half-brothers who had the same father, each claiming to be the firstborn, which caused each to believe he was the ruling deity. This conflict is thought to be the source of many later conflicts between the gods.

etheric: Etheric pertains to an environment that is not based on physical reality but still contains energetic form. Many ideas or thoughtforms in the etheric may become manifest in the physical world.

Eve: Eve was the first female prototype created from the cloning or gene splicing of the male humanoid prototype called Adam. This pertains to *Homo sapiens* only.

Founders: The Founders are the collective soul or energy of the humanoid family. To physical beings they manifest in humanoid form—tall, graceful, androgynous—appearing somewhat insect-like. Humanity is the result of the internal fragmentation of the Founders.

Frequency: Matter is vibrating energy. Different vibratory rates denote the properties of matter. Frequency is the rate at which molecules or consciousness vibrates.

future selves: Because the past, present, and future exist simultaneously, beings may contact parts of themselves across the expanse of time. Extraterrestrials will often contact their past selves (such as Earth humans) to create a connection, and this can often heal their own past. The idea of "higher selves" and "future selves" can sometimes be interchangeable in that a future self is an evolved version of the present or past self.

galactic family: The galactic family is the group of extraterrestrial beings (physical and nonphysical) who are interrelated energetically and/or physically with Earth's development. These include: the Lyran races, Arcturus, Sirius, the Pleiadian races, Zeta Reticuli, Orion, and many others not mentioned.

Homo: *Homo* (Latin for "man") denotes a genus of the order of primates that includes all races of modern man (*Homo sapiens*) and various extinct species.

Homo sapiens: *Homo sapiens* is the single surviving species of human evolutionary development, or modern man, belonging to the genus *Homo* and the primate family Hominidae. The account in Genesis of the creation of man refers to the creation of *Homo sapiens*, not of other extinct species such as Neanderthal.

human: *Webster's* defines "human" as "akin to humus, the ground; having the qualities or attributes of man." This can be expanded by saying that the term "human" refers specifically to the Earth human, who is a subset of the larger humanoid family of the Lyran forefathers.

humanoid: Humanoid as used in the text refers to anyone of Lyran descent.

hybrid: A hybrid is anything derived from heterogeneous sources or composed of elements of different or incongruous kinds. The hybrids spoken of in UFO literature are primarily a cross between the Earth human and Zeta Reticuli beings. The specific process that is used to create these hybrids has not yet been revealed. It uses not only genetic splicing and cloning but a form of light-plasma engineering technology with which humans are unfamiliar.

id: Freud defines the id as being the part of the personality structure that is primitive, instinctual, childish, and obeys the pleasure principle. The qualities of the id can be likened to the humans' passage through second-density reality in the early stages of life.

illuminati: *Webster's* defines "illuminati" as "people possessing, or alleging to possess, superior enlightenment; a name for various sects or societies that claim to possess superior enlightenment." This may refer to humans as well as various extraterrestrial groups (physical or nonphysical) who are either self-deluded or who deliberately attempt to gain control of human society. Some such negative groups may include: Orions, Sirians, Lyrans, and renegade Pleiadians. The historical foundation of the Illuminati is rooted in times past when various extraterrestrial groups were in control (or fighting for control) of Earth in whole or in part. Because of these ancient interactions, the illuminati believe that they have territorial rights over Earth that they still disagree about among themselves. Some will attempt incarnation in order to carry out their wishes in the physical. The illuminati can also be viewed from the nonphysical as an archetypal energy that once interacted physically with Earth. This group eventually side-stepped natural evolution and became a specifically focused archetype. This archetype is bound tightly with the planet by its need to keep humans from their natural evolutionary processes.

incarnate: The act of incarnation (as the term is used) is the process whereby a soul will embody itself in a physical vehicle in a separative density such as the third or fourth. The created illusion is that there is a memory loss of the greater identity of an individual consciousness.

inception: The term "inception" is used in the text to denote the beginning point of *Homo sapiens* on Earth.

Isis: In ancient Egypt, Isis was known as the wife/sister of Osiris, sister of Nephthys, and mother of Horus. She is featured prominently in Egyptian mythology as a goddess of immense magical power and as the archetypal maternal figure. Other cultures have known her as Ishtar (Semites), Athena (Greeks), Kwan Yin (Chinese), and Inanna (Sumerians).

karma: Karma denotes balance and is a principle carried within the soul's energy from lifetime to lifetime. It is simply the nature of energy. The old way of understanding was that karma was balanced through "an eye for an eye." Contemporary Indian yogi Amrit Desai defines karma as "the experience of unresolved, incomplete experiences of the past, returning again and again in the present, giving us new opportunities to encounter it consciously and resolve it." Karma can be carried by an individual, a group, a species, or a mass consciousness.

Lemuria: Lemuria was a continent and a cultural period that predated and overlapped Atlantis. It was located in the Pacific region of Earth and is thought to have been the first culture influenced by extraterrestrial sources.

lenticular clouds: Lenticular clouds have the form of a double convex lens or a lentil. Often their breathtaking appearance is similar to a saucer-shaped spacecraft. Although nature is often behind such a cloud formation, sometimes the physical environment will translate extraterrestrial energy or consciousness into this form.

Lyra: The constellation of Lyra has long been recognized in Earth's mythology. Some have even connected it with the Pleiades. For example, Ovid, who mentioned that the seven strings of Lyra equaled the number of the Pleiades. This can be considered the birthplace or womb of the humanoid race within Earth's area of the Milky Way. All subspecies such as Sirians, Orions, Earth/Terrans, Pleiadians, Vegans, Zeta Reticuli, Centaurians, Altairians (and many lesser-known groups) are descendants of the Lyran races.

Lyran group: The Lyran group is referred to as the original seeders of humanoid life on Earth. The text refers to Lyrans as being the forefather race of other groups such as the Pleiadians and Sirians, as well as being the first physical fragmentation from the Founders of Life.

macrocosm: Macrocosm refers to a large-scale model of a smaller unit. An example is the solar system representing the structure of atomic particles.

mass consciousness: Mass consciousness refers to the singular identity of a group. For example, the mass consciousness of Earth is made up of each individual consciousness integrated into a homogeneous unit.

matrix: (from Latin: *mater/mother*) A matrix is that which originates, develops, or encloses anything; a network of ideas that forms a symbiotic relationship; an archetypal template.

Meier, (Billy) Eduard: The Swiss man Billy Meier is known to possess the most extensive contact notes from repeated interactions with Pleiadian beings, among others. Numerous photographs have been taken that clearly show spacecraft in detail.

Men in Black: Also known as "MIBs," these beings are known as terrorizers of UFO contactees. They are described as being tall and wearing dark clothing. They have been seen with slightly oriental features and often wear dark glasses. Their apparent purpose is to frighten contactees into silence about their experiences and knowledge. Originally thought to be government agents, other ideas have presently surfaced such as: thoughtforms, androids, and negatively oriented extraterrestrials (Orions, Sirians, and Grays). One or all of the above ideas (in various combinations) can be correlated with the MIB identity. Since the original publishing of this text, the comedy movie *Men in Black* was released in the late 1990s, and portrayed these beings as some kind of intergalactic police. While the movie was a comedy, it certainly provides some food for thought.

meta-atomic: Meta-atomic refers to the idea of beyond subatomic. The template that defines the subatomic nature exists on a meta-atomic level.

microcosm: Microcosm means anything regarded as a world in miniature. An example of this is how atomic structure relates to the structure of the solar system.

multidimensional: A multidimensional idea is one that possesses many dimensions. Humans are referred to as multidimensional because they exist on many dimensional levels as yet unseen or unmeasurable.

Neanderthal: Neanderthal refers to a paleolithic cave dweller of the late Pleistocene epoch (*Homo neanderthalensis*), whose bones have been found in parts of Europe, Africa, and Asia. The remains of the Neanderthal have been dated as far back as 100,000 years ago. They seem to have evolved out of *Homo erectus* and then died out during the appearance of *Homo sapiens* 35,000 years ago.

Noah: Noah is a Semitic derivative of the much earlier Sumerian name "Utnapishtim" and the Akkadian "Ziusudra." The writings of these civilizations all portray a Noah-like character who is warned of the flood by the god Enki. The Genesis story of the flood is a condensation of much earlier and much more detailed pre-Biblical accounts in Sumerian and Akkadian literature.

octave: Octave is the eighth of seven steps; it is the integration of seven levels. As it is used in the text, it refers to a realm of existence that consciousness will move into after integrating the seven densities.

Orion: The constellation of Orion is a pattern of stars that has intrigued humankind since ancient times. The word "Orion" may derive from the ancient Akkadian word "Uru-anna," which means the "light of heaven." Western cultures have often identified this constellation as the Hunter. The inherent energy of Orion is associated with polarity conflict. Earth is presently attempting a final integration of these polarities, hence the strong feelings of connection that many humans display regarding Orion.

Orion light: The term "Orion light" refers to the point in Orion's evolution where they have succeeded in integrating polarity. It can also be considered the Orion mass consciousness—the nonphysical aspect of Orion that operates from a sense of unity and integration.

Osiris: Osiris is considered one of the principle Egyptian gods. He has been referred to as "he who dwells in Orion with a season in the sky and a season on Earth," among other epithets. Whatever his identity, most ancient writings strongly point to his extraterrestrial origin.

photothermic: Photothermic involves both light and heat. In their underground caverns the Apexians/Zeta Reticuli mutated to convert certain frequencies of light into heat.

photovoltaic: Photovoltaic refers to the idea of providing a source of electric current from light or similar radiation. In the underground caverns, the Apexians/Zeta Reticuli mutated to the point where they could convert certain frequencies of light and radiation into electrical energy.

plasmic energy: As used in the text, plasmic energy is a form of highly condensed, nearly liquid light.

Pleiades: The Pleiades group is an open star cluster in the constellation Taurus, existing approximately 500 light-years from Earth. There are 250–500 stars within the cluster, although only nine have been named. Most ancient cultures claim seven stars. These include China, who called them the "Seven Sisters of Industry," and Greece, who referred to them as the "Seven Daughters of Atlas." More than any other star group, the Pleiades has captured the attention of both ancient and modern civilizations.

polarity/polarization: Polarity refers to the presence or manifestation of two opposite (or contrasting) principles or tendencies. Polarization is the production of the state of polarity, where rays of light or energy exhibit different properties in different directions.

prism: A prism is a transparent body with a triangular base used to polarize or decompose light or energy into its spectrum.

Prism of Lyra: This is the archetypal idea of the entrance of consciousness into this reality. For Earth's galactic family, the entrance point exists within the Lyran system. As consciousness energy emerged, it fragmented into seven density frequencies, much as a prism would fragment light into seven visible colors.

Prototype: A prototype is an original model on which something is formed; an archetype; a form on which a group is based. In the text, the term/name "Adam" is used to denote the prototype on which *Homo sapiens* is based.

Reticuli: As used in the text, Reticuli refers to the beings from the star system Zeta Reticuli.

Reticulum Rhomboidalis: This star group lies north of Hydrus and the Greater Cloud and contains thirty-four stars of magnitudes from 3.3 to 7. The star system of Zeta Reticuli 1 and Zeta Reticuli 2 are present in this formation and are seen only from the Southern Hemisphere of Earth.

Science of Chaos: The study of apparent random motion that reveals a much deeper level of order below the superficial observation is referred to as the Science of Chaos.

Semjase: Semjase was the name of the female Pleiadian cosmonaut who served as Billy Meier's primary contact.

Set: (Also spelled as: Seth, Setekh, Setesh, Suty, or Sutekh.) Generally speaking, in Egyptian mythology Set is seen as the god of chaotic forces and violence. There has been considerable controversy over his actual role in ancient Egypt. The temples and priesthoods of Set are mentioned in the text in reference to the worship of dark forces.

Sirian Group: As used in the text, the Sirian group refers to a group of extraterrestrials (not necessarily all from Sirius) who were instrumental in the inception of Earth and the development of the human race.

Sirius: Sirius, known as the Dog Star, is a member of the constellation Canis Major. It lies 8.7 light-years from Earth and is the most brilliant star (as distinguished from planets) observed by the naked eye.

social memory complex: This term refers to a mass consciousness or a nonphysical group-matrix identity that has evolved from a physical society.

soul braiding: A soul braid is the most common form of what has been labeled "walk-in." It occurs when physical individuals take in more of their own higher, future, or parallel energy and incorporate it into their own personalities and physiological lives.

Sumerian: The Sumerians were a people who comprised one of Earth's oldest known civilizations (approximately 4000 B.C.), located in southern Mesopotamia (Iraq/Iran). They were a non-Semitic people of unknown origin. They claimed to have had the foundation of their civilization given to them by the "DIN.GIR" —pure ones of the bright-pointed objects, or people of the fiery rockets—or, in human terms, extraterrestrials.

superego: Freud defined the superego as a system within the mind that, acting consciously or unconsciously, brings perceived parental, social, or moral standards to bear on the actions and decisions of the ego. As used in the text, the superego is equated with the higher aspect of consciousness that is the nexus for the integration of personality.

time: Time can be considered a specific continuum where the relationship of movement and speed are measured through linear means.

Tree of the Knowledge of Good and Evil: Referred to in the book of Genesis, it is the tree in the Garden of Eden whose fruit God forbade Adam and Eve to eat. As used in the text, the tree of the knowledge of good and evil symbolizes the knowledge of polarity.

Tree of Life: In the book of Genesis, Adam and Eve were banished from Eden and forbidden to eat from the tree of life, which would give them immortality. As used in the text, the tree of life represents knowledge of the divine relationship between human beings and the Creator, thus revealing that our spirituality is not dependent on those who genetically engineered us.

Vega: Vega is the alpha star in the constellation of Lyra (even though it is actually closer to Earth than it is to the other star systems in the Lyran constellation). Vega was one of the first Lyran civilizations to develop a unique and cohesive identity that assisted in seeding and colonizing many systems, including Altair, Centauri, Sirius, and Orion.

Walk-In: Generally, a walk-in experience will take two forms. The most common can be considered a soul braid in which more of an individual's own energy (higher self or future aspects) is brought in and integrated with the personality. The second and more rare is an instance in which an actual "separate" consciousness inhabits a human body while the original soul departs the physical plane. This is a highly personal experience where the newly arrived entity does not need to proclaim its origin or status. Quite frequently the soul-braid experience is mistaken for the walk-in exchange because the personality construct (as biochemically encoded within the brain) experiences much the same manifestation in either case.

white hole: As used in the text, a white hole is an emergence point for consciousness and energy.

Zeta Reticuli: Discovered in the late 1960s, these two stars are located in the Reticulum constellation, which is seen from Earth's Southern Hemisphere. As used in the text, the Reticuli are a race with many subgroups who are conducting the primary genetic experiments and abductions on present-day Earth humans. Their average height is three and one-half feet. They have large craniums and extremely large eyes. Their sex is indistinguishable. Overall their intent is benign, despite the trauma that many individuals experience in their presence.

Selected Bibliography

Anka, Darryl. *The New Metaphysics.* Light and Sound Communications, 1986.

Burnham Jr., Robert. *Burnham's Celestial Handbook, Vols. 1, 2, and 3.* Dover Publications, 1978.

Cott, Jonathan. *The Search for Omm Sety.* Doubleday, 1987.

Dickinson, Terence. *The Zeta Reticuli Incident.* AstroMedia Corp., 1976.

Ellis, Normandi. *Awakening Osiris: The Egyptian Book of the Dead.* Phanes Press, 1988.

Fix, William R. *Star Maps.* Octopus Books, 1979.

Freer, Neil. *Breaking the Godspell.* Falcon Press, 1987.

Fuller, John G. The *Interrupted Journey.* The Dial Press, 1966.

Grant, Joan. *Eyes of Horus.* Ariel Press, 1942.

Hart, George. *Dictionary of Egyptian Gods and Goddesses.* Routledge & Kegan Paul, 1986.

Jung, Carl. *Man and His Symbols.* Dell Publishing, 1964.

Kinder, Gary. *Light-years.* Atlantic Monthly Press, 1987.

Krupp, E.C. *Echoes of the Ancient Skies: The Astronomy of Lost Civilizations.* New American Library, 1983.

McConnell, James V. *Understanding Human Behavior, Second Edition.* Holt, Rinehart & Winston, 1977.

Moody, Raymond. *Life After Life.* Stackpole Books, 1976.

Royal, Lyssa. *The Arcturus Connection*, audiotape. Royal Priest Research, 1989.

Royal, Lyssa. *The Sirius Connection*, audiotape. Royal Priest Research, 1989.

Royal, Lyssa. *Lyra and the Pleiades*, audiotape. Royal Priest Research, 1990.

Royal, Lyssa. *Pleiadian Ancestry*, audiotape. Royal Priest Research, 1989.

Royal, Lyssa. *The Orion Conflict*, audiotape. Royal Priest Research, 1989.

Royal, Lyssa. *Zeta Reticuli Visitors*, audiotape. Royal Priest Research, 1989.

Royal, Lyssa. *History of the Zeta Reticuli*, audiotape. Royal Priest Research, 1989.

Royal, Lyssa. *The Association of Worlds*, audiotape. Royal Priest Research, 1989.

Royal, Lyssa. *Earth Inception*, audiotape. Royal Priest Research, 1989.

Sitchin, Zecharia. *The Stairway to Heaven*. Avon Books, 1985.

Sitchin, Zecharia. *The Twelfth Planet*. Avon Books, 1976.

Sitchin, Zecharia. *The Wars of Gods and Men*. Avon Books, 1985.

Strieber, Whitley. *Communion*. William Morrow, 1987.

Temple, Robert K.G. *The Sirius Mystery*. Destiny Books, 1976.

Wolkstein, D. and Kramer, S.N. *Inanna: Queen of Heaven and Earth*. Harper and Row, 1983.

Wood, David. *Genisis: The First Book of Revelations*. The Baton Press, 1985.

Zeilik, Michael. *Astronomy: The Evolving Universe*. Harper & Row, 1979.

Reference Materials:

New American Standard Bible. Thomas Nelson Publishers, 1960.

Holy Bible, New International Version. Zondervaan Publishers, 1978.

The Living Webster Encyclopedic Dictionary of the English Language. English Language Institute of America, 1977.

About the Authors

Lyssa Royal Holt holds a B.A. in psychology and is an internationally known channel and lecturer from Arizona. In 1979 she had a clear UFO sighting with her family that triggered a profound interest in extraterrestrial phenomenon. This experience led to a series of dreams in which she was told that she would be a channel. Lyssa studied channeling in depth in Los Angeles and developed her natural talents before beginning to channel publicly in 1985. Since then she has traveled worldwide, giving seminars and sacred site tours. She is the co-author of a number of books (published in many languages) including *Visitors from Within, Preparing for Contact,* and *Millennium: Tools for the Coming Changes,* as well as the *Galactic Heritage Cards,* a divination system of 108 cards. She has been seen on numerous national and international television shows, including the Discovery Channel. Though Lyssa often works with extraterrestrial information through her channeling, the practical application of her channeled information is of utmost priority to her. She is both a student and teacher of yoga as well. Currently, she lives in Arizona with her husband Ronald Holt. Her website is **www.lyssaroyal.com.**

Keith Priest is an independent researcher and co-author of Royal Priest Research's books *Visitors from Within* and *Preparing for Contact.* Through his research, he has delved into ancient languages, biblical studies, anthropology, and history. He combines those studies with astronomy, mythology, and psychology. Though he has never seen an extraterrestrial spacecraft—much less an extraterrestrial!—his studies have shown him that the extraterrestrial issue not only fits nicely into all these areas, but is in fact an integral piece of the puzzle that may connect them all.

THE
GALACTIC HERITAGE CARDS
with Booklet

by Lyssa Royal

$29.⁹⁵

ISBN 978-1-891824-88-3
108 cards

For more than 20 years, students from around the world have asked Lyssa Royal how to understand their personal galactic heritage and star connections, and how this knowledge can be applied to their lives on Earth. We could provide no direct assistance except for workshops and channeling sessions on tape, until now.

In 2010 Lyssa, together with the multidimensional consciousness that she channels called Germane, began to fulfill a longtime dream -- the creation of a set of divination cards to help seekers unlock the awareness of their star connections and how to apply this wisdom to their present life now in a grounded, practical way. Together with the amazing transformational art of Hong Kong film director and visual artist David Cow, this system is the first and only one of its kind.

The overall concept of the cards is to explore the journey from unity to fragmentation and polarity, and back to reintegration. Since each of us is part of the same one consciousness, this is a journey that unifies us all. The components of the cards explore this journey in a variety of ways, such as through the species or star system depicted, the time stream, the card lesson, and even the artwork itself. There is an underlying image that spans all the cards when they are laid out on a grid. This underlying image represents our journey back to integration, so each card, when separated from the whole deck, carries the energy of that underlying truth of our journey through the stars as we return Home.

𝔶 *Light Technology* PUBLISHING

PREPARING FOR CONTACT

A Metamorphosis of Consciousness

by Lyssa Royal and Keith Priest

"Clearly written with all terminology defined, Preparing for Contact is an excellent introduction for those readers who are unfamiliar with ET phenomena. " —Body Mind Spirit Magazine

"Lyssa Royal's research has 'unearthed' a breathtaking volume on interspecies communication and its relationship to the human consciousness." —Light of Consciousness Magazine

"Preparing for Contact is a book that is both timely and therapeutic..." —Dr. Leo Sprinkle, Ph.D., Counseling Psychologist

✦ ✦ ✦

ET contact is happening now. We may not remember it clearly. We may think it is only a dream. We may ignore the signs of ET contact simply because we do not understand them. And most of all, we may simply be too frightened to fully acknowledge its presence.

This ground-breaking book is a combination of narrative, precisely-focused channeled material from Lyssa and personal accounts. An inside look at the ET contact experience is given, including what the human consciousness experiences during contact with an extraterrestrial. How do our perceptions of reality change during contact? How can we learn to remember our contact experiences more clearly?

As you journey through the pages of this book you will also take an inner journey through your own psyche and discover a whole new dimension to your unexplained experiences. Join us on the path of transformation as humankind begins . . .

$16.⁹⁵

ISBN 978-1-891824-90-6

☽ ULTIMATE UFO SERIES

Superchannel Robert Shapiro can communicate with any personality anywhere and anywhen. He has been a professional channel for over twenty-five years and channels with an exceptionally clear and profound connection.

ANDROMEDA

The Andromedans and Zoosh through Robert Shapiro

Now the Andromedans who originally contacted the Professor speak through superchannel Robert Shapiro and again give instructions that will allow trained scientists to construct a shield around existing Earth planes so that Earth astronauts can fly to Mars or to the stars.

The Andromedans also tell what really happened on their journeys and on Earth, and they clear up questions one would have after reading the English or Spanish version of the previous book—the text of which follows the channeling in this book. In addition, they supply a lively account of their lives on their home planet in the Andromedan constellation of our galaxy.

$16⁹⁵ SOFTCOVER 450 P.
ISBN: 1-891824-35-X
978-1-897824-35-1

- They Share Advanced Science with a Mexican Professor, a Physicist.
- They Share Details of Their Interaction with a Devastating Nuclear Explosion Involving Two Countries on Earth.
- The Physicist Is Later Committed to a Mental Institution and Then Disappears Forever. His Journals Also Disappear.

The eight-foot-tall, highly mental crew members of the ship who speak:

- Leia, the beautiful Cultural Specialist and Social Diplomat who so intrigued the Professor
- Cheswa, the Cultural Liason
- G-dansa, Leia's daughter, equivalent to an eight-year-old ET Eloise
- Duszan, the Junior Scientist

- Onzo, the Senior Scientist and Crew Leader, the youngest, yet genetically modified to be the most brilliant of the crew
- Playmate, a two-foot-tall, roly-poly Andromedan who teaches communion of heart and mind.

CHAPTER TITLES INCLUDE:

Our Ancestors Came from Space
Extraterrestrial Concepts of Energy
Reviewing the Past and Feelings
Early Visits to Earth
Antimatter
Our Explosive Atmosphere
On Space Travel
ET View of Our Religion
Life and Death of Planets
Changes Overcome Me
The Extraterrestrial Photographed

Phone: 928-526-1345 or 1-800-450-0985 • Fax: 923-714-1132

🜨 *Light Technology* PUBLISHING

ASTROLOGY:
PLANET PERSONALITIES & SIGNS
SPEAK THROUGH ROBERT SHAPIRO

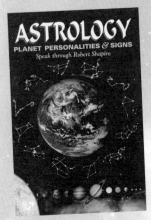

12 PLANETS • 12 SIGNS
4 NEW PLANETS AND 1 NEW SIGN
THE THIRTEENTH SIGN AND A PLANET
TO BALANCE MOTHER EARTH

The Planets and Signs of Astrology speak
to us through superchannel Robert Shapiro
—sharing not only **LONG-LOST**
INFORMATION but also **NEW WAYS**
OF BEING for an awakening humanity.

CHAPTER TITLES

Isis and the Sun	Venus	Mother Earth	Libra
The Sun	Mercury	Virgo	The 13th Sign
The Moon	Mars	Gemini	Capricorn
Chon-Deh, Sun Helper	Unknown Planet	Etcheta	Cancer
Saturn	Planet Axis	Pisces	Scorpio
Jupiter	Isis	Taurus	The 10th Planet
Pluto	Uranus	Aquarius	The 11th Planet
Neptune	Seeker—Milky Way	Leo	The 12th Plnet
Astrology Expert	Astrological Historian	Sagittarius	Teacher of Astrology
		Aries	Reveals the Mysteries

As the Planets and Signs speak through Robert, their personality traits
and interests, many of which have been unknown since ancient times, can
be clearly heard and felt. In addition, you—humanity—have made such
progress that other new energies and traits of the Planets and Signs are
expressed through their words. These energies, traits and characteristics
were only potential in earlier times but now are becoming available to
you to become aware of and to express within your life on Earth as you
awaken to your natural self.

$29⁹⁵
Plus Shipping

ISBN 978-1-891824-81-4
700 P. Est. Softcover
6 x 9 Perfect Bound

Visit our online bookstore: www.LightTechnology.com

COMING SOON

WALK-INS

Now Natural, Benovelent Birth Is Available on Earth

through Robert Shapiro

Pre-publication Price

$19⁹⁵

Plus Shipping

Regular Price

$25⁰⁰

Plus Shipping

ISBN 978-1-891824-40-1
Softcover 500+ pp.
6 X 9 Perfect Bound

This book is intended to be practical advice for day-to-day living for people who know they are walk-ins, for people who believe they might be walk-ins, for the family and friends and business associates of people who are believed to be walk-ins or may believe they are walk-ins themselves. In short, this book is intended to serve the community to understand the walk-in phenomenon and for those who are experiencing it personally, to be able to apply it in such a way as they are able to live easier, more comfortable, more useful, and more fulfilling lives.

—REVEALS THE MYSTERY through Robert Shapiro

Phone: 928-526-1345 or 1-800-450-0985 • Fax: 923-714-1132

ANIMAL SOULS SPEAK

THROUGH ROBERT SHAPIRO

Robert Shapiro is largely known as a professional trance channel, with several series of published books such as *The Explorer Race* Series, of which this is book #13; *Shining the Light* Series (8); *Shamanic Secrets* Series (3); *Benevolent Magic*, and the *Ultimate UFO* Series.

But, as he is now, he is a mystical man with shamanic capabilities well and thoroughly infused into him. He also has many unusual skills that he is teaching through blogs, the *Sedona Journal of Emergence* and these books. It is his intention to bring about the most benevolent change available on the planet through sharing his personal inspirations as well as his channeling, which in this book is of these wonderful beings humans call animals.

Robert Shapiro

Chapters Include:

Eel	Deer	Phoenix	Dog	Myna Bird	Ant
Tortoise	Elephant	Chickadee	Whale	Llama	Moss
Frog	Rabbit	Koala Bear	Shark	Sea Sand	Overspirit
Skunk	Polar Bear	Spider	Gnat	Giraffe	Human Sea Elder
Snail	Earthworm	Cat	Butterfly	Manta Ray	Creator's Emissary

The animal world will speak, if you prefer, through elders. This has certain advantages, since that way they can include knowledge and wisdom to a degree—not to a vast degree, but to a degree—about their home planets.

—Grandfather

Each animal brings a wonderous gift to share with humanity—enjoy it!

Welcome to the footsteps of the loving beings who support you, who wish to reveal more about themselves to you and who welcome you, not only to planet Earth, but more specifically to the pathway of self-discovery. Take note as you read this book of what resonates, what stimulates your own memories. Use it to inspire you, to encourage you, to support you along your path toward inevitable self-discovery, and ultimately to support self-discovery in others that results in revealing the true and most benevolent heart of all beings. Good life.

—Creator's Emissary

The Explorer Race Series

$29.⁹⁵   ISBN 1-891824-50-3
Softcover, 640 p.

Visit our online bookstore: www.LightTechnology.com

PLANT SOULS SPEAK
A NEW WAY OF INTERACTING WITH PLANTS

"What we intend to speak about—if I may speak in general for all plants—is how you can interact with plants in a more benevolent way for you as the human species. For a long time, you have been clear on medicinal uses of leaves and stems and seeds and flower petals and so on, but you are only getting about one-tenth of the energy available to you that way. It is always better to interact with the plant and its energies in its live form, but you need to know how.

"The intention of this book is to reveal that formula so that you can stop searching, as a human race, for the magical cures to diseases by exhausting the supply of life forms around you, when a much simpler process is available. This book will not just comment on things you know about but show you what you are missing in your interaction with plants."

—Dandelion

$16.^{95}$

ISBN 978-1-891824-74-6
Softcover, 286 pp.

Chapters Include:

Cherry Tree	Maple Tree	Palm Tree	Peach Tree
Pine Tree	Redwood	Walnut Tree	Brown Rice
Crabgrass	Oat Grass	Wetland Grass	Angelica
Bamboo	Corn	Daffodil	Dandelion
Hibiscus	Holly	Ivy	Kelp
Marijuana	Orchid	Rose	Sage
Soy Bean	White Rose		

𝕵 *Light Technology* PUBLISHING

ET Visitors Speak Vol. 1

through Robert Shapiro

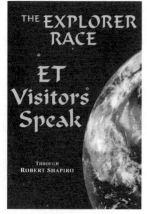

ven as you are searching the sky for extraterrestrials and their spaceships, ETs are here on planet Earth—they are stranded, visiting, exploring, studying the culture, healing Earth of trauma brought on by irresponsible mining, or researching the history of Christianity over the last 2,000 years. Some are in human guise, some are in spirit form, some look like what we call animals, as they come from the species' home planet and interact with those of their fellow beings we have labeled cats or cows or elephants. Some are brilliant cosmic mathematicians with a sense of humor presently here as penguins; some are fledgling diplomats training for future postings on Earth when we have ET embassies. In this book, these fascinating beings share their thoughts, origins, and purposes for being here.

$14.95

310 PP. SOFTCOVER
ISBN 979-1-891824-28-8

- *A Sentient Redwood*
- *Qua on Mormonism*
- *A Warrior of Light, the Ultimate Ally*
- *Penguins: Humorous Mathematicians*
- *Xri from the Ninth Dimension*

- *Observer Helps Cats Accomplish Their Purpose: Initiating Humans*
- The Creation and Preparation of the Resource Specialists' Ships
- *. . . and many, many more!*

ET Visitors Speak Vol. 2

through Robert Shapiro

or those of you who've always wanted to meet somebody completely different, here's your opportunity. This book contains the continuing adventures of visitors to planet Earth. In a strange sense, you might include yourself as one of those, as the human race does not really claim the title of full-time and permanent Earth citizen. So when you're reading this book, think about it as if you were visiting another planet. What would you say in reaction to the local population, their habits, and so on? Put yourself in the picture so this isn't just a meaningless travel log from various beings that you don't know and may never meet. Make it personal this time because the time is coming, maybe even in some of your lifetimes, when you might just be one of those extraterrestrials on another planet. So you might as well practice now and get your lines down right.

$19.95

500 PP. SOFTCOVER
ISBN 978-1-891824-78-4

- *ET from a Future Version of Saturn*
- *Tuwass, a Visitor to Future Earth*
- *Xzhetah, ET Hybrid*
- *Visitor from Planet Odin*
- *The Sound of Breath*

- *ET Visitor from Orion*
- *Tsong Ti from the Pleiades*
- *Time-Loop Traveler*
- *Antiquarian, Pleiadian Teacher*
- *. . . and many many more!*

Shamanic Secrets Mastery Series

Speaks of Many Truths and Reveals the Mysteries through Robert Shapiro

Shamanic Secrets for Material Mastery

This book explores the heart and soul connection between humans and Mother Earth. Through that intimacy, miracles of healing and expanded awareness can flourish. To heal the planet and be healed as well, we can lovingly extend our energy selves out to the mountains and rivers and intimately bond with the Earth. Gestures and vision can activate our hearts to return us to a healthy, caring relationship with the land we live on. The character of some of Earth's most powerful features is explored and understood, with exercises given to connect us with those places. As we project our love and healing energy there, we help the Earth to heal from human destruction of the planet and its atmosphere. Dozens of photographs, maps and drawings assist the process in twenty-five chapters, which cover the Earth's more critical locations.

498 p. $19.95 ISBN 978-1-891824-12-8

Shamanic Secrets for Physical Mastery

Learn to understand the sacred nature of your own physical body and some of the magnificent gifts it offers you. When you work with your physical body in these new ways, you will discover not only its sacredness, but how it is compatible with Mother Earth, the animals, the plants, even the nearby planets, all of which you now recognize as being sacred in nature. It is important to feel the value of oneself physically before one can have any lasting physical impact on the world. If a physical energy does not feel good about itself, it will usually be resolved; other physical or spiritual energies will dissolve it because it is unnatural. The better you feel about your physical self when you do the work in the previous book as well as this one and the one to follow, the greater and more lasting will be the benevolent effect on your life, on the lives of those around you and ultimately on your planet and universe.

576 p. $25.00 ISBN 978-1-891824-29-5

Shamanic Secrets for Spiritual Mastery

Spiritual mastery encompasses many different means to assimilate and be assimilated by the wisdom, feelings, flow, warmth, function and application of all beings in your world that you will actually contact in some way. A lot of spiritual mastery has been covered in different bits and pieces throughout all the books we've done. My approach to spiritual mastery, though, will be as grounded as possible in things that people on Earth can use— but it won't include the broad spectrum of spiritual mastery, like levitation and invisibility. I'm trying to teach you things that you can actually use and benefit from. My life is basically going to represent your needs, and it gets out the secrets that have been held back in a storylike fashion, so that it is more interesting."

—Speaks of Many Truths through Robert Shapiro

768 p. $29.95 ISBN 978-1-891824-58-6

Phone: 928-526-1345 or 1-800-450-0985 • Fax: 923-714-1132

⚘ *Light Technology* PUBLISHING

THE EXPLORER RACE SERIES

ZOOSH AND HIS FRIENDS THROUGH ROBERT SHAPIRO

THE SERIES: Humans—creators-in-training—have a purpose and destiny so heartwarmingly, profoundly glorious that it is almost unbelievable from our present dimensional perspective. Humans are great lightbeings from beyond this creation, gaining experience in dense physicality. This truth about the great human genetic experiment of the Explorer Race and the mechanics of creation is being revealed for the first time by Zoosh and his friends through superchannel Robert Shapiro. These books read like adventure stories as we follow the clues from this creation that we live in out to the Council of Creators and beyond.

❶ THE EXPLORER RACE

You individuals reading this are truly a result of the genetic experiment on Earth. You are beings who uphold the principles of the Explorer Race. The information in this book is designed to show you who you are and give you an evolutionary understanding of your past that will help you now. The key to empowerment in these days is to not know everything about your past, but to know what will help you now. Your number-one function right now is your status of Creator apprentice, which you have achieved through years and lifetimes of sweat. You are constantly being given responsibilities by the Creator that would normally be things that Creator would do. The responsibility and the destiny of the Explorer Race is not only to explore, but to create. 574 P. $25.00 ISBN 0-929385-38-1

❷ ETs and the EXPLORER RACE

In this book, Robert channels Joopah, a Zeta Reticulan now in the ninth dimension who continues the story of the great experiment—the Explorer Race—from the perspective of his civilization. The Zetas would have been humanity's future selves had not humanity re-created the past and changed the future. 237 P. $14.95 ISBN 0-929385-79-9

❸ EXPLORER RACE: ORIGINS and the NEXT 50 YEARS

This volume has so much information about who we are and where we came from—the source of male and female beings, the war of the sexes, the beginning of the linear mind, feelings, the origin of souls—it is a treasure trove. In addition, there is a section that relates to our near future—how the rise of global corporations and politics affects our future, how to use benevolent magic as a force of creation and how we will go out to the stars and affect other civilizations. Astounding information. 339 P. $14.95 ISBN 0-929385-95-0

❹ EXPLORER RACE: CREATORS and FRIENDS
The MECHANICS of CREATION

Now that you have a greater understanding of who you are in the larger sense, it is necessary to remind you of where you came from, the true magnificence of your being. You must understand that you are creators-in-training, and yet you were once a portion of Creator. One could certainly say, without being magnanimous, that you are still a portion of Creator, yet you are training for the individual responsibility of being a creator, to give your Creator a coffee break. This book will allow you to understand the vaster qualities and help you remember the nature of the desires that drive any creator, the responsibilities to which a creator must answer, the reaction a creator must have to consequences and the ultimate reward of any creator. 435 P. $19.95 ISBN 1-891824-01-5

❺ EXPLORER RACE: PARTICLE PERSONALITIES

All around you in every moment you are surrounded by the most magical and mystical beings. They are too small for you to see as single individuals, but in groups you know them as the physical matter of your daily life. Particles who might be considered either atoms or portions of atoms consciously view the vast spectrum of reality yet also have a sense of personal memory like your own linear memory. These particles remember where they have been and what they have done in their infinitely long lives. Some of the particles we hear from are Gold, Mountain Lion, Liquid Light, Uranium, the Great Pyramid's Capstone, This Orb's Boundary, Ice and Ninth-Dimensional Fire. 237 P. $14.95 ISBN 0-929385-97-7

❻ EXPLORER RACE and BEYOND

With a better idea of how creation works, we go back to the Creator's advisers and receive deeper and more profound explanations of the roots of the Explorer Race. The liquid Domain and the Double Diamond portal share lessons given to the roots on their way to meet the Creator of this universe, and finally the roots speak of their origins and their incomprehensibly long journey here. 360 P. $14.95 ISBN 1-891824-06-6

THE EXPLORER RACE SERIES

ZOOSH AND HIS FRIENDS THROUGH ROBERT SHAPIRO

➐ EXPLORER RACE: The COUNCIL of CREATORS

The thirteen core members of the Council of Creators discuss their adventures in coming to awareness of themselves and their journeys on the way to the Council on this level. They discuss the advice and oversight they offer to all creators, including the Creator of this local universe. These beings are wise, witty and joyous, and their stories of Love's Creation create an expansion of our concepts as we realize that we live in an expanded, multiple-level reality. 237 P. $14.95 ISBN 1-891824-13-9

➑ EXPLORER RACE and ISIS

This is an amazing book! It has priestess training, Shamanic training, Isis's adventures with Explorer Race beings—before Earth and on Earth—and an incredibly expanded explanation of the dynamics of the Explorer Race. Isis is the prototypal loving, nurturing, guiding feminine being, the focus of feminine energy. She has the ability to expand limited thinking without making people with limited beliefs feel uncomfortable. She is a fantastic storyteller, and all of her stories are teaching stories. If you care about who you are, why you are here, where you are going and what life is all about—pick up this book. You won't lay it down until you are through, and then you will want more. 317 P. $14.95 ISBN 1-891824-11-2

➒ EXPLORER RACE and JESUS

The core personality of that being known on the Earth as Jesus, along with his students and friends, describes with clarity and love his life and teaching two thousand years ago. He states that his teaching is for all people of all races in all countries. Jesus announces here for the first time that he and two others, Buddha and Mohammed, will return to Earth from their place of being in the near future, and a fourth being, a child already born now on Earth, will become a teacher and prepare humanity for their return. So heartwarming and interesting, you won't want to put it down. 354 P. $16.95 ISBN 1-891824-14-7

➓ EXPLORER RACE: Earth History and Lost Civilization

Speaks of Many Truths and Zoosh, through Robert Shapiro, explain that planet Earth, the only water planet in this solar system, is on loan from Sirius as a home and school for humanity, the Explorer Race. Earth's recorded history goes back only a few thousand years, its archaeological history a few thousand more. Now this book opens up as if a light was on in the darkness, and we see the incredible panorama of brave souls coming from other planets to settle on different parts of Earth. We watch the origins of tribal groups and the rise and fall of civilizations, and we can begin to understand the source of the wondrous diversity of plants, animals and humans that we enjoy here on beautiful Mother Earth. 310 P. $14.95 ISBN 1-891824-20-1

⓫ EXPLORER RACE: ET VISITORS SPEAK

Even as you are searching the sky for extraterrestrials and their spaceships, ETs are here on planet Earth—they are stranded, visiting, exploring, studying the culture, healing the Earth of trauma brought on by irresponsible mining or researching the history of Christianity over the past two thousand years. Some are in human guise, and some are in spirit form. Some look like what we call animals as they come from the species' home planet and interact with their fellow beings—those beings that we have labeled cats or cows or elephants. Some are brilliant cosmic mathematicians with a sense of humor; they are presently living here as penguins. Some are fledgling diplomats training for future postings on Earth when we have ET embassies here. In this book, these fascinating beings share their thoughts, origins and purposes for being here. 350 P. $14.95 ISBN 1-891824-28-7

⓬ EXPLORER RACE: Techniques for GENERATING SAFETY

Wouldn't you like to generate safety so you could go wherever you need to go and do whatever you need to do in a benevolent, safe and loving way for yourself? Learn safety as a radiated environment that will allow you to gently take the step into the new timeline, into a benevolent future and away from a negative past. 208 P. $9.95 ISBN 1-891824-26-0

⚜ *Light Technology* PUBLISHING

TIME AND THE
TRANSITION TO NATURAL TIME

THE EXPLORER RACE

TIME

AND THE **Transition to Natural Time**

THROUGH **ROBERT SHAPIRO**

$16.⁹⁵

ISBN 978-1-891824-74-6
Softcover, 286 pp.

"The purpose of this book is to provide a context for your lives in the sequence you find yourselves in now. This explanation of time—and, to a degree, its variables—is being provided for you so that you will understand more about your true, natural, native personalities and so that you will be reminded that you are, as you know, in a school and that this school is purely temporary.

You don't come here very often to this place of linear time; like your own human lives, you are in school for only so long, and then you live your lives. When you exist beyond this school, you will find all those lives infinitely easier, and even as the Creator, your lives will be easier than they are in their single, linear lives that you're living now, because you will have all your components."

—Founder of Time

Chapters Include:

Visit our online bookstore: www.LightTechnology.com

✤ Light Technology PUBLISHING

ULTIMATE UFO SERIES

The ZETAS

History, Hybrids, and Human Contacts

THROUGH Robert Shaprio

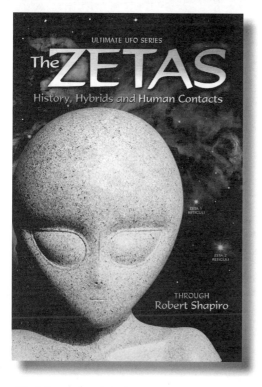

The Zetas Speak About:

- Betty Andreasson, the Hills and the Ceremony of Renewal
- Children of Isis: Path of the Zeta
- Describing the Zetas
- The Zetas in Human History
- The Truth of Travis Walton's Case, Among Others, and the Planet of Cats
- Gifted Spacecraft, Crashed Spacecraft and the Test of Technology
- Roswell and the Case of Billy Meier
- The Effects of Time Travel
- Parent Race of Zeta
- Creation of the Zetas
- Earth's Work with Quantum Mastery and the Loop of Time
- Joao and the Andromedans
- The Pascagoula Affair

$25⁰⁰
Plus Shipping

ISBN 978-1-891824-36-4
Softcover 435 pp.
6 X 9 Perfect Bound

"The beings on Zeta Reticuli are the future selves—granted, several million years into the future—of the beings on Earth right now. On the soul line, this has to do with your evolution to become more, to be more established benevolently on a creative level. By the time your souls become those Zeta Reticulian beings several million years into the future, you will be able to interact with all life in the most benevolent way while being strongly intellectual and scientific.

In this way, your science will have a complete balance with heart and soul. This is one of the greatest aspects of significance between you and the Zeta Reticulian beings as of this time. So to them you are their past lives—that's why they're so fascinated with you—but for you, when you interact with these beings, you are truly meeting, in many senses, your future."

— Zoosh through Robert Shapiro

Phone: 928-526-1345 or 1-800-450-0985 • Fax: 923-714-1132

THE ANCIENT SECRET OF THE FLOWER OF LIFE
VOLUME 1

O nce, all life in the universe knew the Flower of Life as the creation pattern— the geometrical design leading us into and out of physical existence. Then, from a very high state of consciousness, we fell into darkness, the secret hidden for thousands of years, encoded in the cells of all life.

Now we are rising from the darkness and a new dawn is streaming through the windows of perception. This book is one of those windows. Drunvalo Melchizedek presents in text and graphics the Flower of Life Workshop, illuminating the mysteries of how we came to be.

Sacred Geometry is the form beneath our being and points to a divine order in our reality. We can follow that order from the invisible atom to the infinite stars, finding ourselves at each step. The information here is one path, but between the lines and drawings lie the feminine gems of intuitive understanding. You might see them sparkle around some of these provocative ideas:

- Remembering Our Ancient Past
- The Secret of the Flower Unfolds
- The Darker Side of Our Present and Past
- The Geometries of the Human Body
- When Evolution Crashed, and the Christ Grid Arose
- Egypt's Role in the Evolution of Consciousness
- The Significance of Shape and Structure

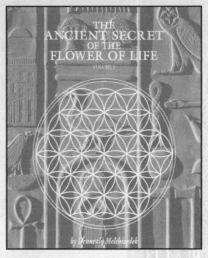

$25⁰⁰ Softcover 228 P.
ISBN 1-891824-17-1

Available from your favorite bookstore or:

LIGHT TECHNOLOGY PUBLISHING
PO Box 3540 • Flagstaff, AZ 86003

Drunvalo Melchizedek's life experience reads like an encyclopedia of breakthroughs in human endeavor. He studied physics and art at the University of California at Berkeley, but he feels that his most important education came after college. In the past 25 years, he has studied with over 70 teachers from all belief systems and religious understandings.

For some time now, he has been bringing his vision to the world through the Flower of Life program and the Mer-Ka-Ba meditation. This teaching encompasses every area of human understanding, explores the development of humankind from ancient civilizations to the present time and offers clarity regarding the world's state of consciousness and what is needed for a smooth and easy transition into the 21st century.

Visit our online bookstore: www.LightTechnology.com

THE ANCIENT SECRET
OF THE FLOWER OF LIFE
VOLUME 2

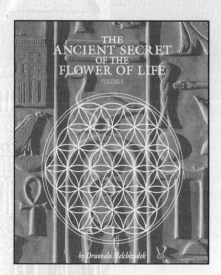

$25⁰⁰ Softcover 252 P.
ISBN 1-891824-21-X

- The Unfolding of the Third Informational System
- Whispers from Our Ancient Heritage
- Unveiling the Mer-ka-ba Meditation
- Using Your Mer-ka-ba
- Connecting to the Levels of Self
- Two Cosmic Experiments
- What We May Expect in the Forthcoming Dimensional Shift

 Available from your favorite bookstore or:

LIGHT TECHNOLOGY PUBLISHING
PO Box 3540 • Flagstaff, AZ 86003

The sacred Flower of Life pattern, the primary geometric generator of all physical form, is explored in even more depth in this volume, the second half of the famed Flower of Life workshop. The proportions of the human body, the nuances of human consciousness, the sizes and distances of the stars, planets and moons, even the creations of humankind, are all shown to reflect their origins in this beautiful and divine image. Through an intricate and detailed geometrical mapping, Drunvalo Melchizedek shows how the seemingly simple design of the Flower of Life contains the genesis of our entire third-dimensional existence.

From the pyramids and mysteries of Egypt to the new race of Indigo children, Drunvalo presents the sacred geometries of the Reality and the subtle energies that shape our world. We are led through a divinely inspired labyrinth of science and stories, logic and coincidence, on a path of remembering where we come from and the wonder and magic of who we are.

Finally, for the first time in print, Drunvalo shares the instructions for the Mer-Ka-Ba meditation, step-by-step techniques for the re-creation of the energy field of the evolved human, which is the key to ascension and the next dimensional world. If done from love, this ancient process of breathing prana opens up for us a world of tantalizing possibility in this dimension, from protective powers to the healing of oneself, of others and even of the planet.

Phone: 928-526-1345 or 1-800-450-0985 • Fax: 923-714-1132

Light Technology PUBLISHING

SEDONA
Journal of EMERGENCE!

Rated Number One!
We Offer Answers to Satisfy the Heart and to Inspire Lives!

YOU ARE EXPERIENCING AN UNPRECEDENTED EXPANSION

into a new reality and a dimensional shift into a new state of being. This movement from one dimension to another while in a physical body has never been done before—it feels like you are building the rocket you're riding while it is blasting off!

THERE ARE NO ANCIENT BOOKS, NO RULEBOOKS, no manuals or procedures, no record of how to do this thing, because it has never been done before. During previous dimensional shifts, embodied beings would die in the old reality and then be reborn in the new one in new bodies with a different vibrational frequency.

SO LIGHTBEINGS, THROUGH THEIR CHANNELS, EXPLAIN THIS PROCESS and offer guidance and spiritual techniques to help you learn to feel and express love and benevolence—and to encourage you to change your behavior to ensure that the Earth remains habitable while you expand into your natural self and awaken to your natural talents and abilities. As this happens, you will allow yourself to flow with all humanity into a more benevolent version of Earth—into another dimensional focus, another of the strata of this existence.

The Sedona Journal of EMERGENCE! is the one monthly magazine readers never throw away.

Get SPECIAL UPDATES of channeled material before they're available on the newsstand with ELECTRONIC SUBSCRIPTIONS!

ELECTRONIC SUBSCRIPTIONS available for SJE!

$29⁰⁰/YEAR for 12 months anywhere on the planet! **$55⁰⁰** for 2 years!

Must be puchased online at: www. sedonajournal.com for you to obtain a user name and password.

Get the latest channeling and astrology 2 weeks before it is available on the newsstand.

Visit our online bookstore: www.LightTechnology.com

☥ *Light Technology* PUBLISHING ✦ 159

SEDONA
Journal of EMERGENCE!

👉 **ORDER NOW!**
TO RECEIVE SPECTACULAR SAVINGS!

ORDER ONLINE!
SAVE expensive freight or postage on your Sedona Journal subscription

We are now making
ELECTRONIC SUBSCRIPTIONS
available for the
SEDONA JOURNAL OF EMERGENCE!
We have now added content that will not fit into the printed magazine!

• Get the entire Journal online by subscription—and get it 2 weeks before it goes on the newstand!

• Save on expensive freight or postage on your Sedona Journal subscription!

Electronic Subscriptions

❏ 1 yr. . . . .$29 ❏ 2 yr. $55

All Electronic and Combo Subscriptions *MUST* be purchased online at:
www.sedonajournal.com
to obtain username and password

Get the Best of Both Worlds!
Special Combo Offers!
U.S.A
Get a Printed Subscription Along with an Electronic Subscription - U.S.A. only

1st Class ❏ 1 yr. . . $82   ❏ 2 yr. . . $159
2nd Class ❏ 1 yr. . . $59   ❏ 2 yr. . . $109

Canada & Mexico
Get an Airmail Printed Subscription Along with an Electronic Subscription for only
❏ 1 yr. . . . $95   ❏ 2 yr. . . . $179

NOTE: The U.S. Postal Service has changed postal rates, eliminating Canadian 2nd Class Surface and increasing all airmail rates.

All Countries
Except U.S.A., Canada, & Mexico
Get an Airmail Printed Subscription Along with an Electronic Subscription for only
❏ 1 yr. . . . $152   ❏ 2 yr. . . . $285

NOTE: The U.S. Postal Service has changed postal rates, eliminating global 2nd Class Surface and increasing all airmail rates.

---

yes! Send Me:

Printed and Mailed Subcriptions

1ST CLASS	2ND CLASS
❏ 2 yrs. $129	❏ 2 yrs. $79
❏ 1 yr. $65	❏ 1 yr. $43

🇺🇸

CANADA & MEXICO
AIR
❏ 2 yrs (24 issues) $149
❏ 1 yr (12 issues). $79
U.S. dollars only

NOTE: The US Postal Service has changed postal rates, eliminating Canadian 2nd Class Surface and increasing all airmail rates.

ALL COUNTRIES
Except USA, Canada & Mexico
AIR
❏ 2 yrs (24 issues) $255
❏ 1 yr (12 issues). $136
U.S. dollars only

NOTE: The US Postal Service has changed postal rates, eliminating global 2nd Class Surface and increasing all airmail rates.

My Name _____
Address _____
City _____ State: _____
Zip:_____ Phone _____
Email _____
Gift Recipient Name _____
Address _____
City _____ State: _____
Zip:_____
Personalized Gift Card from_____
METHOD OF PAYMENT:

❏ CHECK #   ❏ M.O.

❏ VISA   ❏ MASTERCARD   ❏ NOVUS   ❏ AMEX

CARD NO._____
EXPIRATION DATE _____
SIGNATURE _____

Phone: 928-526-1345 or 1-800-450-0985 • Fax: 923-714-1132

♦ **Light Technology** PUBLISHING

EASY ORDER 24 HOURS A DAY

Visit Our Websites!

Order ONLINE!
www.lighttechnology.com
Email:
customersrv@
lighttechnology.net

✴ Shopping Cart w/ Secure Transactions
✴ In-Depth Information on Books, Including Excerpts and Contents
✴ Use our Great Links to Other Sites

Order by Mail
Send To:
Light Technology Publishing
PO Box 3540
Flagstaff, AZ 86003

CHANNELS • PREDICTIONS • FEATURES
SEDONA Journal of EMERGENCE!
Peace to All Beings

✴ Read Excerpts of Monthly Channeling and Predictions in Advance
✴ Use Our Email Links to Contact Us or Send a Submission
✴ Electronic Subscriptions Available—With or Without Print Copies

Order by Phone
800-450-0985
928-526-1345

BENEVOLENT MAGIC
& Living Prayer
Ancient Secrets of Feminine Science

Learn the techniques of benevolence toward self and benevolence toward others and you will create global peace. Download all the techniques of benevolent magic and living prayer for FREE!

Order by Fax
928-714-1132

The **EXPLORER RACE** SERIES

All of humanity constitutes the Explorer Race, volunteers for a grand and glorious experiment. Discover your purpose, your history and your future. Download the first chapter of each book for FREE!

Available from your favorite bookstore or:

Shamanic Secrets
For Material, Physical & Spiritual Mastery

What we call shamanism is the natural way of life for beings on other planets. Learn to be aware of your natural self and your natural talents and abilities. Download the first chapter of each book for FREE!

Visit our online bookstore: www.LightTechnology.com